Mankind's Last Chance

Healing for a Broken World

Mankind's Last Chance

Healing for a Broken World

Richard Poole

BOOKS

Winchester, UK
Washington, USA

First published by O-Books, 2013
O-Books is an imprint of John Hunt Publishing Ltd., Laurel House, Station Approach,
Alresford, Hants, SO24 9JH, UK
office1@jhpbooks.net
www.johnhuntpublishing.com

For distributor details and how to order please visit the 'Ordering' section on our website.

ISBN: 978 1 78279 106 5

A CIP catalogue record for this book is available from the British Library.

Design: Stuart Davies

The views and opinions expressed in this book are exclusively those of the author
for which he accepts full responsibility.

Printed and bound by CPI Group (UK) Ltd, Croydon, CR0 4YY

We operate a distinctive and ethical publishing philosophy in all
areas of our business, from our global network of authors to
production and worldwide distribution.

DEDICATION

To all people everywhere.

SPECIAL THANKS

My special thanks go to Catherine and Desiree,
and to Peter Hardwick.

ACKNOWLEDGEMENTS

With much appreciation to Sir Douglas and
Lady Ruskin who are always there, to Alice who told
me not to quit whatever the circumstances,
and to Linda who encouraged me to take up my pen.

PREFACE

A number of things came together to prompt the writing of this book. The first was a decision to retire from a lifetime in humanitarian work that had been forced upon me. I had not felt ready to retire in the sense that my health was still good and my commitment to the humanitarian cause was still as strong as ever, yet it seemed that one door after another was suddenly being closed to me and this after a working life of nearly forty years in which one wonderful door of opportunity had opened effortlessly and perfectly onto another. It seemed that the Great Being into whose hands I had commended myself many years before might possibly be trying to tell me something.

At the same time a sense of foreboding that I had since childhood about the state of the world and which I had always kept to myself was now crystallising inside me with a force that was telling me that it was time to do something about it and that the time was now. The realisation that this hidden feeling that I had not even dared to acknowledge was valid and that I no longer had to keep it concealed came to the fore.

The worsening state of our economic crisis served to confirm my growing fears for the world while filling me with disgust that it should have been caused by so much greed and irresponsibility at a time when the world was crying out for generosity and compassion. Had the world learnt nothing from the past hundred years? I asked myself.

All the while I heard supposed 'experts' talk endlessly about and around the crisis but without ever coming up with any relevant answers, neither to our economic situation nor our deteriorating natural environment. A voice inside cried out, 'now is the time to speak and to speak loud and clear and straight from the heart for nothing else matters and there is not a moment to lose'. From the moment the decision to write the book was taken in November 2011 it has felt as if my life has been leading up to this moment, as if everything I had ever done had been a preparation for this task.

Then an unexpected gift landed in my lap and revealed to me what was going on. From out of nowhere I was asked by an organisation I had previously worked for to go to Rwanda for a few months to manage a camp of 19,000 Congolese refugees. I hesitated for a while thinking that it might interfere with the completion of the book but then I realised that I could do both; I could return to my beloved Africa and also finish my book while overlooking the beautiful Lake Kivu.

The short visit to Rwanda showed me two things: the first was that the momentum to write and complete the book had taken over my whole life in such a fashion that I was barely conscious of the book's content or the time passing. And the second was that, profound though my love for Africa still is, I knew that my time as a humanitarian worker really was at an end and that whatever days I have left on this earth must be devoted to some other cause. It was still not entirely clear what this cause might be but whatever it was it would be with the interests of the human race at heart but without the practicalities of organising health clinics, food supplies and water and sanitation facilities. I was so grateful for these months in Rwanda because they reassured me that I was now back on the right track and that I should not look back.

My passion to continue serving my fellow men and women has only intensified over recent months. I have no wish now other than to get the message of *Mankind's Last Chance* out into the public domain as fast as possible. The crisis that I have sensed and feared since my childhood is now with us and is writ large across the heavens and is calling to be broadcast far and wide. This is the aim of this book. To direct all those who are willing to listen to the spiritual path that can alone lead us through our present crisis to safety. This and only this will suffice. All else will merely add to the chaos.

FOREWORD

Richard Poole draws upon his life's experience as a humanitarian worker and as a student of world religions to bring us this intriguing book. He addresses the three foremost issues of our day – the global economic crisis, our deteriorating natural environment, and the meaning of life in a rapidly changing world. He sees a common thread linking all three and argues that only a return to the spiritual path can bring a solution to our collective malaise.

He challenges what he believes are the three great myths of our time: the myth that truth is exclusively accessible through the intellect; the myth that humanity moves forward as a result of the influence of human genius; and the myth that freedom and the satisfaction of desire are the foundation of happiness.

I found *Mankind's Last Chance* moving and thought-provoking. Do I personally buy his argument? I do not honestly know – part of me hopes that he is right and part of me hopes that he is wrong, especially in his assessment of the calamity that awaits us if we do not put our house in order quickly.

What I do know from an acquaintanceship that spans four decades is that Richard Poole is a person of strong conviction and unwavering commitment to whatever cause he undertakes. My contention is that it would be unwise to dismiss what he has to say without carefully listening to the arguments and weighing the evidence.

Dr. Peter Hardwick

INTRODUCTION

I have written a couple of books, three to be precise, and all of them have been anecdotal in nature recounting my experiences as a humanitarian worker with real people in real situations in Latin America and Africa. I have never had any inclination to join the ranks of those who like to dwell extensively on their own condition. I spent four years at university contemplating the self-indulgent ramblings of twentieth century intellectuals such as Sartre, Camus and Ionesco and it left me with feelings of despair. Their disease had been contagious. Better not wallow in misery for the sake of it, I told myself, better wait until you can do something about it. My interest had never been to study disease but to cure it.

Having said all this and having vowed that my third book would be my last I now find myself reaching for my pen contrary to expectation and the promise that I made. The reason for it is that I believe the world is about to go through the greatest crisis it has ever faced and I feel that I have something to offer. Pretentious, you may think, but it is not really so. More pretentious would it be to say that there is no solution to the crisis for this would presume all knowledge. All I am saying is that I believe that there is a solution to our predicament and that I would like to put it forward for consideration. It may well be the only thing that I know, or think I know, and I am happy with this. I no longer harbour pretentions to be an intellectual - no thanks, I have had my fill of such things.

Our planet is in pain and in urgent need of healing, both people and matter. Our current economic crisis and the degradation of the environment are merely symptoms of a much deeper malaise which this book will seek to identify and address. If all goes well we will emerge from it – the book, I mean - with a clear idea of what the problem is and how to resolve it.

The book is in two parts: the first, which is entitled 'The Problem', considers our present predicament and how we reached it; and the second, which is entitled 'A Solution', considers what we might do to put things right. I have broken down the first part which is much longer into three sections to make it more manageable for the reader.

You may have already noted that the tone is somewhat informal. This may be the product of my passing years or it may be the product of the urgency that our crisis generates. In any case I sense that time is too short for beating about the bush and I prefer to get straight to the point. I have also chosen to keep the chapters relatively short. I personally prefer to receive other people's thoughts in this fashion and I suspect that the reader may prefer the same. Neither would I wish to engage in abstruse arguments that run the risk of tiring and confusing everyone, myself included.

I have chosen to punctuate the narrative with reminiscences from my field experience. I have done this for several reasons: firstly, to provide evidential support for a point that I am making; secondly, to underscore the universality of the human condition; and thirdly, to add the odd bit of light relief here and there. We should never take ourselves too seriously I have recently concluded, after a lifetime of doing exactly the opposite.

If *Mankind's Last Chance* has any structure to it at all it is circular rather than linear which means that unlike the previous books which were episodic in character with one event following the other in chronological order, this time we shall be revisiting topics that have already been addressed and developing them further. I would request, therefore, that the reader kindly refrain from thinking to himself 'he has already said this, why is he saying it again?' There will be a method to the movement, I promise, the repetition being no more than an aide-memoire that will allow us to move onto other things.

Colchester, June 2012

CONTENTS

PART 1

THE PROBLEM

SECTION 1

WHERE HAVE WE GONE WRONG?

Chapter One

A WORLD IN TURMOIL

I was born into a world that I knew was in trouble from the moment I could think and I switched off from it, somehow aware even at this early age that it was terminally flawed. My mother took me to the doctor when I was six years old because she thought I was going deaf. The doctor, a canny Irishman by the name of H. Leader O'Sullivan, stood me over in a corner and whispered a few words in my direction and then asked me what he had said. I was too frightened of his authority to pretend that I had not heard and so I answered him correctly. 'Don't worry, Mrs. Poole', he told my mother gently, 'he's just playing the 'old soldier'. And so I was. Just as an old soldier might want to screen out certain things that he would rather forget so I was screening out the world around me. I did not like it at all.

Today the fault lines of our decline are even more visible and they are growing wider and deeper by the day. This is true of most places but for the moment I will speak only of Britain for despite having spent some thirty-odd years working in different parts of the world this is still far and away the country that I know best.

Most people in Britain today are given to self-destruction although few of us seem to see it. The older ones among us probably do as we look back over our years and reflect on the way things used to be and how we have fared in our unique opportunity to contribute to this miraculous existence of ours, ever mindful that we could and should have done better. Many of us, like me, will be found shaking our heads in disbelief at the way things have gone, our hopes of a peaceful sunset dashed by an erosion of values that has exceeded our worst fears and we now find ourselves frustrated by an inability to communicate what we have learned to others who are beyond reach.

The rank and file, those who are busily engaged with the daily act of living, appear to be reasonably content with the way things are and see no reason to change beyond the odd gesture like reducing calories, recycling household waste or buying a more fuel efficient car. And even if they did, the daily routine allows little space for radical transformation. The younger generation, buoyed no doubt with the confidence that comes with youth, seem sure that they are on the right track and that availing themselves of whatever life has to offer is all part of the journey. The notion that they might possibly be heading in the wrong direction is unlikely to occur to them.

Many fail to see a connection between the freedom that we have been taught to revere and the increasing pull of our many appetites for food, alcohol, sex, fashion, entertainment, gambling and so forth. 'More of the same' seems to be the mantra as we implicitly trust that 'enough' will one day bring happiness. Neither do we have the patience to wait. Our concentration span is no longer measured by the time that it takes to learn a new skill, or to read a book, or to follow a test match but by the time that it takes to watch a movie, play a video game, eat a pizza, drink a lager or tell a joke. It has to be instant, it has to be effortless, and it has to feel good.

This surfeit of indulgence is in no small part the product of a joint assault on our senses by those branches of the media that trade in the superficial, in particular the movie and the advertising industries which know only too well how to promote fantasy and appeal to our egos. Their world of falsehood is paralleled by the less seductive but also problematical world of the news industry led by the tabloid newspapers which routinely simplify and distort the news they report, delight in scare-mongering and specialise in cutting others down to size. Both sides of the industry are harmful in their own way, the one for creating expectations that cannot be met and the other for depressing morale.

Whatever their function may have been in the past, and it may have been noble, neither serves the common good today, although no doubt each would defend the integrity of its motives and its methods to the very end.

There is often a time lag between our actions and the results they produce such that we may not see a connection between the two. This is true of our relationships with those who are closest to us and it is even more so where the wider community is concerned. For well over a generation now, perhaps two, we have been subjected to a media assault that has ridden roughshod over virtually everything that was formerly considered decent and necessary for our collective well-being. And all the while life has appeared to carry on the same, thereby proving, or so it seemed, that society can function quite well without a moral compass and that the prophets of doom were wrong.

It has always been possible to sustain this position as long as a majority of us have been reasonably comfortable, our health has been good and we have felt secure inside our own homes. We may have heard of others who were less fortunate and who were living on the edge, people who had precious little to eat and nowhere to live and who were forever on the run and living in fear, but it was others and not us, and it was usually somewhere remote and so we were able to push it from our minds. It did not affect us personally and so we continued about our daily business, no doubt saddened by the images that we saw but without feeling any immediate compulsion to intervene.

With economic collapse on a massive scale now looming and the air around us becoming warmer and more contaminated by the day many of us are beginning to sense that we may not be quite so far removed from tragedy as we once thought. There is a growing feeling that things are not as they should be and that it may no longer be just a minority of us who are affected. Concomitant with this feeling of unease is a nagging suspicion that we ourselves are somehow responsible. These two sets of feelings, unease and responsibility, are finding expression in an upsurge of political and social activism as increasing numbers of angry and frustrated people take to pointing fingers and demanding corrective action, only to discover that our ship is proving more difficult to turn than anyone had imagined.

There are others, of course, who are quick to deny that the changes in our economic and natural environments are serious and that they themselves might possibly be to blame if they were; and to a certain extent they will be right in the sense that there may never have been any malice aforethought on their part. They may say, for example, that the hole in the ozone layer, or the declining value of the euro, or the wretched working conditions of labourers in the mines of the Congo and the sweatshops of Bangladesh are not the result of anything that they personally have done and that all they have been doing is sitting quietly at home in front of the television minding their own business. And they may sincerely believe that what they say is true. The reality is quite different, however, because there is every connection between the life that each one of us leads, wherever he happens to be and whatever he happens to be doing, and what is going on elsewhere in the world, right down to the very last detail. It is one of the purposes of this book to explain what this connection is.

Nonetheless, cracks are appearing in the composure of ordinary people, the sort who would normally have soldiered on regardless with courage and resolve, and a good many are becoming nervous. Ironically, it is these same cracks that give cause for hope because they may well provide the opportunity for sanity to creep back into our lives. This is certainly my own hope because I see an urgent need for sanity to return to Britain en masse and I have made it the primary purpose of this book to help this process along. In fact the book is intended as a wake-up call to the nation, a plea to all of us to stop what we are doing and take stock of where we are.

I have seen societies collapse in Africa and I have written about it in a book entitled *The Day of the Dragon*. The book which was written in the heat of anger at the international community's failure to intervene in Rwanda, Sierra Leone and Liberia, predicted the London riots of 2011 (which threaten to return in a far more virulent form by the way) and mentions in passing that the euro is not a credible currency, a subject that is addressed at some length in a future chapter. It is a terrifying experience to be in a place when law and order breaks down and it is not something that is confined to impoverished third world countries. It can happen anywhere and anytime that standards of decency fail.

It is my belief that Britain is in such a state right now and that it is poised, along with the rest of the world, to descend into chaos. The threat is as real and as potentially destructive as the Second World War was to Europe or a Third World War would be to our planet. The only difference this time is that the enemy is within instead of without, for we, ourselves, are the enemy. It does not necessarily have to happen like this because there are a number of different forces at work some of which are positive and one of these is having the effect of bringing the peoples of the world closer together in a common purpose like never before. If this leads to a full recognition of our interdependence as a species and an appreciation of the intrinsic worth of each one of us as individuals, then we shall be heading in the right direction and the outcome will be good. But it demands that immediate corrective action be taken and this in turn demands that we each assume the mantle of responsibility and play our due part.

I believe passionately in the good sense of the British people and in our capacity to respond in right measure when called upon to do so. We usually take a while to get started but once we do we tend to make a pretty good job of things. Were I not to believe this in my innermost being I would not be spending long hours at my computer writing these words. The message is simple and it is this – if we are to avoid the descent into chaos of which I speak then we need to act and we need to act quickly, for time is short, desperately short, and there is not a moment to lose.

I invite you to accompany me on a journey of discovery that will seek to explore the precise nature of the crisis that we are now facing and to explain what we, as a nation and as a race, might do to mitigate and even correct its worst effects. To do this properly we shall need first to go back in time to the place where we started. In fact we shall need to go right back to the very beginning of our existence and follow again the path that brought us to where we are now.

Chapter Two

RETRACING OUR STEPS

I have always had a great fondness for animals but I have always seen them for what they appeared to me to be rather than as extensions of myself; I have never been given to anthropomorphism. I have never felt that dolphins and chimpanzees, for example, were gifted with any special intelligence - heightened instinct, perhaps, but not intelligence.

A moment of insight came some years ago when I was watching a programme on television about chimpanzees – 'our nearest relatives' as some evolutionary biologists like to call them. One poor specimen had caught its hand in a snare that had been set by a poacher and was frantically pulling at it to get free. We did not see it, fortunately, but the narrator assured us that in such situations it is quite normal for a chimpanzee to keep pulling until the hand is completely severed. This tragic episode came just a few minutes after the same narrator had been extolling what he believed was the chimpanzee's innate intelligence.

What struck me forcibly about this incident was the realisation that a human being in the same situation would have, a) stopped deliberately hurting himself, and b) worked out that if he were to loosen the snare with his other hand and pull it in an opposite direction he might find a way of escape. And what struck me with equal force was the realisation that if we were to return one million years from now we would still find chimpanzees frantically pulling their hands in the wrong direction at the risk of losing a limb. In other words they would have learned nothing from the experience.

I saw with crystal clarity in that moment that we human beings have a faculty that sets us apart from the animal kingdom and that this faculty is the ability to think in abstract.

We have, in other words, an intellect that is capable of operating outside the domain of the senses. Because of it, although we are by nature earth-bound creatures the same as chimpanzees, we are able to fly through the air and travel across and even under the water. Chimpanzees, on the other hand, along with all other animal species, are prisoners of their innate condition. They are denied this faculty which is unique to humankind. Herein lies the difference between the two and it is a difference of immeasurable significance for it is a difference not of degree but of condition. In brief, as must be patently clear even to a child, chimpanzees will never acquire the ability to think in abstract, not in a million years, not even in the life-span of our sun on which all earthly life depends. It is not going to happen.

Having established that we human beings have a faculty of reason that sets us apart from animals and allows us to escape the constraints of our natural condition we may now consider some of its implications. One of the major ones is that with it comes a measure of responsibility for we have within us the capacity to enhance or diminish our human condition; that is, we can make it or break it in accordance with our will. Recent history has provided us with multiple examples of both possibilities.

Concomitant with the notion of responsibility goes the notion of free will for how else could we be responsible for our actions unless we have free-will? A lion cannot be held responsible for bringing starvation to its pride by eating the last gazelle on the plain since all it is doing is behaving the way that a lion is programmed to behave; it hunts when it is hungry, it has no choice. It does not first count the number of gazelle in the vicinity, calculate how long his stock will last, and then ration itself accordingly. We, on the other hand, have an intellect and can consider the consequences of our actions and this opens up a whole new dimension, that of social responsibility, towards ourselves and others.

I have no interest in engaging in some fruitless debate at

this point concerning the nature of free-will. I spent too many hours in my university days arguing against its existence to go back over it again now. As far as I am concerned the mere fact that we are able to deny the existence of free will is proof enough that it exists for how else could we deny it? I am therefore taking its existence as given. That we human beings have a rational faculty as well as the freedom to apply it is the foundation on which all else depends. There is no other reason for our existence. We know this intuitively which is why our art and our literature are ever preoccupied with the meaning of life. As the American writer Kurt Vonnegut Jr. so neatly put it:

Tiger got to hunt
Bird got to fly
Man got to sit and wonder 'Why, why, why'
Tiger got to sleep
Bird got to land
Man got to tell himself he understand.

What I would like to do now is to trace in the broadest of strokes the trajectory of mankind's evolution from its origins in the womb of the world to the present day. We shall need this perspective if we are to grasp the full dimension of our current predicament and what we might do to resolve it.

There are four levels of existence and all of them reflect life in one form or another. They are the mineral, the vegetable, the animal and the human. The mineral lives though the power of the cohesion of its particles that will one day disintegrate. The vegetable possesses this same power of cohesion but in addition it possesses the power of growth and regeneration, all of which will one day cease to exist. The animal possesses these same powers of cohesion, growth and regeneration, in addition to which it possesses the faculties of the senses and the ability to move, all of which will one day disappear. Humanity possesses all of the aforementioned faculties and powers, and in addition to these, as we have just seen, it possesses an intellect the primary characteristic of which is the ability to think in abstract. In so far as this human condition contains within it all the characteristics of the other levels of existence as well as a unique faculty all of its own, it may be said to be the culmination of everything that exists. Humanity is able to contemplate everything in existence from a privileged position, including its own self, which seems little short of miraculous if we stop and think about it.

There is enough archaeological evidence for us to conclude that the earth and its contents were not created in seven days a few thousand years ago but have evolved over millions of years gathering diversity along the way. Whether or not mankind stands alone, or shares a common ancestry with some other species, or indeed with all other species, has yet to be established but let us leave this issue, vital though it is, for the present and agree, if we can, that mankind is sufficiently different from the rest of the contingent world to be considered unique and that whatever evolutionary path he may have taken there is only one human species alive today.

As far as our social organisation goes we appear to have passed though a number of different stages, each one more expansive than the one before, namely, from the family to the clan, from the clan to the tribe, from the tribe to the city state, from the city state to the nation state, and finally to the stage that we are currently about to embrace, from the nation state to the world community. Since no human being, at least to my knowledge, came up with this plan we must assume that unconsciously we have followed some inexorable impulse to arrive at where we are now. There seems to have been a method to its symmetry in that our expansion has always been easier to accept than to reject. In retrospect and in theory we might have been able to resist, had we wanted to, but in reality I suspect that this was not possible. The days of the clan and the tribe, in so far as they can still be said to exist are numbered, while the sovereign powers of nation states are being eroded by the day. That we are now all members of what is commonly referred to as a 'global community', one that embraces every living person on our planet, would appear to be an inescapable fact of life. My contention is that we would do well to recognise this and to make the most of it and that to do otherwise would be folly.

What we have before us, therefore, is a single world community the destiny of which, as we are learning with each passing day, is fully intertwined. We may not have chosen to arrive at this point but, as I am not hearing any complaints from any particular quarter, I suggest that we embrace it and set about organising things to our mutual benefit. We have everything that we need to do so: we have the manpower - that is ourselves; we have the resources of our planet; we have the power of our intellect; and we also have freewill, so in theory there is nothing standing in our way. Just how we might pull all these things together in the right manner constitutes the very purpose of this book and to realise it we shall need to look first at some of the forces that have determined the ebb and flow of our fortunes.

Chapter Three

THE ONE YOU FEED

Although I have spent more than ten years working with Native Americans in Ecuador and Bolivia and have been deeply impressed with their social organisation, their sense of responsibility and their humility I tend to shy away from telling stories about their spirituality because to do so has become something of a cliché. Over the years so many spiritualist mediums have claimed to have spirit guides who were Native Americans, especially chiefs, in their earthly lives that the mere mention of the subject meets with suspicion. As the founder-editor of the renowned magazine Psychic News, Maurice Barbanell, once wryly remarked 'with all these chiefs around one can't help wondering whatever happened to the Indians!' I suspect that the Indian chief may have become fashionable as a spirit guide when people in Europe discovered that the feathered headdress that they wear on ceremonial occasions is a sign of advanced spirituality. It is similar in this regard to the halo found in Christian art, and like the halo in Christian art, which incidentally was often added years later, its true value is to be found in the eye of the beholder.

There is a great deal of misinformation circulating about this theme of Native American spirituality. In the Ecuadorean rainforest there is an ethnic group known as the Shuar who are well-known for a number of reasons, one of them being that they were never conquered by the Spaniards. They were also known for their custom of shrinking the decapitated heads of their enemies and hanging them on poles in their huts. The President of the Shuar Federation with whom I worked for a number of years on a reforestation project would sometimes joke that one of the last heads they shrank about a hundred years ago was that of a European missionary who looked a lot like me.

Within Shuar culture there was, and still is to a small extent, a tradition of taking ayahuasca which is a hallucinogenic plant that is said to allow those who partake of it insight into the spirit world. I have written briefly about this in *The Inca Smiled* and do not wish to repeat myself here. Suffice it to say that American and European hippies, or whatever their modern day equivalent is, have long flocked to the Ecuadorean rainforest to indulge in this hallucinogenic experience. In fact I saw a television documentary on this very subject quite recently, only this time the eager participant was an Australian. What I myself soon learned and what was not made clear in the documentary is that the vast majority of Shuar chose to abandon this traditional practice in favour of Catholic ritual a long time ago and now consider the users of ayahuasca pretty much as we consider alcoholics and drug-addicts in our own culture, namely, as losers and drop-outs who are to be pitied rather than copied.

Another example of European susceptibility to an idealised view of Native American spirituality took place several years earlier when, in Mexico this time and in the company of an aspiring young anthropologist named Richard Luxton, I went to visit a community of Huichol Indians whose head village of San Andres Coamiata is located high up in the Jalisco mountains. Huichol mythology is also based on a hallucinogenic plant, the peyote cactus, the startling colours that it induces being reflected in the colourful designs of Huichol traditional dress.

There was just one flight a week to the village from the local town of Tepic in a small single-engine Cessna airplane. It was a somewhat precarious flight and I had not realised at the time that the bad temper of the pilot before takeoff and during the flight was the product of his fear of crashing. The Huicholis called him 'El Atrevido,' 'The Daring One' on account of the fact that he flew in all conditions and seldom let them down. All the same you had the feeling that it might just be a matter of time before his luck ran out, as it reportedly did for one of his predecessors. Fortunately all went well on this occasion and the pilot duly kept his word to come back and collect us the following week for which he gained my undying gratitude.

After about an hour in the air we descended onto the narrow dirt airstrip, disembarked and started along the dirt path that took us into the village. On the way we came across a raucous, staggering drunk who without preamble grabbed hold of my shirt and demanded that I give him some money which I refused to do. 'Thieving tramp!' I believe I remarked at the time. Later on we discovered that the 'thieving tramp' was none other than the renowned Huichol shaman 'Colas' whom Rick had heard about and had purposely come to meet. We did manage to meet up with him later when he was sober but I never learned if he turned out to be the mine of information that Rick was hoping. I suspect not because they did not spend too much time together.

I did not follow the matter too closely because it was Rick rather than I who was interested in Huichol culture. A powerful intellectual and a gifted academic, Rick already had one eye on a doctoral thesis and was looking for a suitable subject. He had latched onto my spirit of adventure to get to this remote place and this I happened to have over and above any interest in anthropology. My own motivation was always to engage with people of different backgrounds as fellow members of the human race rather than for their cultural trappings. It was an interesting visit and Rick and I made a pretty good team, albeit with differing agendas. He later shifted his attention to the Yucatan and became a mayanologist of considerable renown while Professor of Sociology at the Western New England College in Springfield Massachusetts. He sadly passed away in October 2010.

Despite my longstanding misgivings about quoting Native American seers I have decided to break my own rule and relate to you this very brief and simple tale. I do so because I believe it contains an insight of universal importance. It involves a Cherokee grandfather who is talking to his grandson.

'Inside every human being' starts the grandfather, 'there are two wolves, a good wolf and a bad wolf, and the two are constantly fighting, each one is trying to kill the other one'.

'And which one wins?' asks the grandson.

'The one you feed' replies the grandfather.

This short tale contains within it just about as much as anyone needs to know about the human condition. It contains the story of our history and the story of ourselves. The Aztec symbol of the eagle holding a snake in its talons as seen on Mexican currency and the national flag symbolises the same struggle between good and bad with the eagle as the ethereal power winning. The story of St. George and the Dragon does the same, as does the legend of St. Patrick driving the snakes out of Ireland. The following quotation from a Persian philosopher writing in the early part of the last century illustrates the universality of this same theme:

"There exist in man two powers. One power uplifts him. This is divine attraction, which causes man's elevation. In all grades of existence he will develop through this power. This belongs to the spirit. The other power causes man to descend. This is the animal nature. The first attracts man to the Kingdom. The second brings him down to the contingent world. Now we must consider which of these will gain more power. If the heavenly power overcomes, man will become heavenly, enlightened, merciful; but if the worldly power overcomes, he will be dark, satanic, and like the animal. Therefore he must develop continually. As long as the heavenly power is the greater force, man will ascend."

The teachings of Christianity of course contain this same message of the struggle between good and evil, the one they call God and the other they call Satan. In fact all the world's divine religions contain this same teaching and the difference between them on the matter is so slight as to be of no consequence. I choose to include the word 'divine' at this point because not all belief systems derive from the same source. Some are manmade and have short life-spans. Divine religion is brought to us by one who is recognised by his followers as a messenger of God and who does not claim to be the author of the words he speaks. On the contrary, he states emphatically that his knowledge is not of himself but of the One who sent him. His advent is always in accordance with prophecy and he brings with him a new 'book' that sets out laws and a code of conduct for others to follow.

Within each of us, therefore, there is a higher self and a lower self and there is no common ground between them. They are implacable foes and the one can only exist at the expense of the other. *The lower self*, if we are to define it, is that aspect of our being which is circumscribed by the material world, or that part of us that we share in common with animals. It is characterised by attachment to the world that we see around us and by what we term 'self-interest'. *The higher self* relates to the part of us that we do not share in common with the animals, the distinguishing feature of which is the faculty of reason. This is the aspect of our being that is non-material and operates, as we saw in Chapter Two, beyond the realm of the senses. It is characterised by detachment from the world that we see around us and by what we term 'selflessness'. It is associated with the body but without being part of it. An analogy might be the reflection of the sun in a mirror; the mirror may break but the sun will continue to shine. This is the part of us that is eternal and survives the decomposition of the body.

Most of us will have had experiences at some time in our lives that confirm the existence of the higher self, be it a premonition, an intuition, a dream that foretells a future event, or perhaps what is sometimes referred to as an 'out-of-the-body' experience, and we may also have managed to push it to the back of our minds or even come up with a convenient theory to explain it away. We do this because our modern culture is materialistic in orientation and lacks the terms of reference to account for such experiences adequately. Nonetheless there are other cultures in the world, as I have found everywhere in my travels, that accept such phenomena as perfectly normal and incorporate them into their daily routine without a second thought. In fact it can come as a great surprise to them when they learn that many Europeans do not accept the existence of a spiritual world and are not in regular contact with a Divine Being, nor indeed with their ancestors to whom they themselves often turn in times of need. The spiritual dimension is as obvious and as real to them as the sun and takes about as much effort to see. I suspect that it may have been this way in Europe before we took the material path.

I recall a discussion that I had at one time with a Muslim friend in Khartoum who wished to lend me a book that contained proofs confirming the existence of Allah.

'Do you accept these proofs?' I asked him.

'Yes,' he replied, 'I do, but I don't actually need them. They are really for Europeans, they need such things. We Muslims know it by heart, we do not need convincing'.

The rise and fall of cultures, the same as the rise and fall of individuals, can only be fully understood in terms of the ascendancy of one or the other of the two selves, the higher and the lower. We must constantly bear in mind that the higher self and its attributes mean peace and harmony, while the lower self and its attributes mean division and conflict, so there is a lot at stake. Which of the two gains the ascendancy is a matter that only we as individuals can decide and, as the Cherokee grandfather explains, at bottom it is a question of which of the two we choose to feed. And given that the two wolves are permanently locked in deathly combat we understand that we experiment with our appetites at our peril.

All this may sound somewhat fanciful but in reality it is not. It works like this: someone may decide that he is going to log onto a pornographic site on the internet presumably for sexual excitement and that it is no-one's business but his own. This is not the case, however, because to do so is to feed the lower self which happens to be a ravenous beast whose appetite can never be fully satisfied. In fact to satisfy its appetite in the short term is merely to create an even bigger appetite in the longer term. The lower self is characterised by 'want' which sooner or later becomes 'demand' and demand will exert itself at some point regardless. It has a life of its own and it will take control.

This is the 'Satan' that Christ spoke of but it is within us and not without us. There is no fallen angel prancing around behind the scenes tempting us and trying to cause havoc. Christ never said there was; this is a man-made invention. What I believe he did was to personify the beast within us, which is none other than the lower self, to make it easier for us to identify and to deal with, but the enemy is within us and not without. Mankind has no need of a devil to commit evil; he is quite capable of doing it all by himself. We are the ones who are responsible for our actions, we and we alone. There is a beast within all of us and the more we feed it the more powerful and destructive it becomes. To feed the lower self is a dangerous game, not only for ourselves but for those around us as well because we are all part of a community and our behaviour impacts others.

A conclusion that we might draw from this is that morality is one and that immorality is also one, and that the two possess distinctive natures that respond to distinctive inputs. At some point in our lives we are going to have to decide which of the two selves we are going to espouse, and it has to be one or the other, it cannot be both. It is true that a good many of us, nearly all of us in fact, somehow manage to survive on a daily basis with one foot in either camp, but we will never be fully at peace if we do. It may appear also that certain individuals are able to indulge their every whim and abuse their health at every turn and still lead happy lives, but appearances can be deceptive. What I know from personal experience is that a person will never be truly at peace as long as he has divided loyalties and tries to satisfy two sets of opposing demands. I know this because I have tried it innumerable times and failed.

The implications of the choice we make necessarily take us into the realms of metaphysics. Although I have just said that at some point in our lives we will have to decide which of the two selves we are going to espouse, thereby implying that there is a choice, in reality there is only one option available to us because in the end we will never find peace in submission to the lower self alone and this is because the lower self is destructible whereas the higher self is indestructible. When a person dies and his body goes back to the earth the lower self dies with it, as it must do because the lower self belongs exclusively to the material world. The struggle between the two selves only endures for the time that we are on this earth so that in the end if it is peace and happiness that we are looking for the only place that it can be found is in surrender to the higher self. The individual consciousness of the person that has chosen to identify with the lower self will continue to exist after the disintegration of his body but without having acquired the attributes that pertain to the higher self and which are needed to live a full life in the non-material realm that follows this one. It would be like being born into this world with none of the faculties needed to live a 'normal life'.

Nothing is being said here that has not been said a million times before in churches, temples, mosques, synagogues and religious institutions everywhere. What differences there are, if any, may be found in the choice of terminology and the ecumenical approach but at root it is the same message of the struggle between good and evil, coupled with an acceptance of a nonmaterial dimension that follows this one that we have always heard about. The story does not change.

It is this struggle that gives meaning to our lives and it is one that cannot be ignored because to do so is to capitulate and lose the fight. This has onerous implications for society because no man is an island, nor ever has been, and what any one of us does necessarily impacts those around us. What is making the struggle all the more vital today is the fact that our destiny as a species has become inextricably interconnected in a way and to a degree that has never happened before. Adding to our sense of interconnectedness and making it all the more palpable is the fact that we are able to see it taking place thanks to a revolution in communications technology that beams images from around the world into our homes on a daily basis.

When we talk about 'our neighbours' today we are no longer just talking about those who live in the immediate vicinity but about the entire human race because our modern world, which has rightly been termed a 'global village', has made everyone our neighbour. The implication of all of this, which is truly staggering, is that as a species we look set to either stand or fall as a single entity – and that we may even be able to watch it on television as it happens!

The final outcome is not yet predictable because we are able to influence events. Our destiny even at this late hour still lies within our grasp. We are now sufficiently aware of the extent of our interconnectedness to understand its full import and we also know what we must do to survive. Put in its simplest terms, we must learn to live together in harmony and to do this the beast of our lower nature has to be tamed. This may sound fairly straight forward but given our past record it may not be the easiest task we have ever undertaken.

Chapter Four

CHILDREN

It may seem strange to have a chapter entitled 'Children' in a section that is all about where we have gone wrong but in fact it makes sense. Children are the building blocks of tomorrow's society and if we got it wrong yesterday then it might tell us something about today.

While speaking to a group of businessmen and women about my experiences in Africa a short while ago I made the comment that 'a child in Africa with nothing is infinitely happier than a child in Britain with everything'. A number of people approached me afterwards and asked me to explain why this might be, their curiosity apparently piqued by the thought that our constant striving to do what is right for our children has not brought contentment. As I sought to come up with a meaningful response I realised that a number of the issues had direct relevance to the subject of this book and these I would like to share with you now.

Let me start by relating how I see African children after working with them for some twenty years in the humanitarian field.

African children do not complain and they certainly do not whine. In general their faces are only too ready to explode with joy and laughter at the first opportunity. They are hardworking and respectful of both their parents and elders in general. They do not curse. They are honest and they are generous and they know how to share whatever they have. Those who are fortunate enough to go to school love it. They stand up when the teacher enters the classroom and greet him in unison with 'Good morning teacher!' And they sit in perfect silence paying rapt attention to his every word for the duration of the lesson, whether they are twenty, fifty or eighty in number. At the end of the class when the teacher is about to leave they stand up, again in unison, and say 'Thank you teacher!' And they mean it. Each and every one of them would give their all to have what the very least child in Britain has, namely, a chance to study in a good school without having to pay school fees. And to this we may add - enough to eat, good clothes to wear, a doctor whom they can visit whenever they are sick and medicine if they need it. Such possibilities are beyond their wildest dreams. More likely for them is a life of hardship for which they prepare themselves without complaint, grateful in fact for whatever they have.

The image of African children has suffered greatly as a result of certain humanitarian agencies choosing to depict them as miserable and helpless, which they routinely do for fundraising purposes. They know that when they portray children in this fashion the rich of the world are more likely to put their hands in their pockets and send money. At the same time humanitarian agencies talk endlessly about their efforts to promote 'empowerment' and 'self reliance' when in fact they have never actually achieved it, nor have they even come close to achieving it. In any case it is a myth that Africans are in need of being taught self-reliance. After all, who is more 'reliant' – an African who builds his own house, who grows his own food, who walks everywhere or rides an ancient bicycle, who finds his own medicine from the plants around him and who cleans his teeth with a twig that he cuts from a tree; or a European who owns a house that someone else has built, who buys all his food, who travels everywhere by car, who visits a doctor and obtains medicine from a pharmacy when he is sick, and who cleans his teeth with a toothbrush that probably comes from China?

Africans, both children and adults, are anything but miserable and helpless and to portray them as such is to do them a great disservice. I noted early on in my time in Sub-Saharan Africa that Africans everywhere love to laugh.

At first it can be disconcerting to a European who does not laugh nearly so much and when he does it is often at the expense of someone else, because he may think they are laughing at him but this is seldom the case. Africans laugh because they are joyous and happy people, this much is certain; but they also laugh to lighten their load and to raise their spirits in the face of adversity. They seem to have learned long ago that laughter is the best medicine. In African circles laughter can be an indication of a seriousness of intent and a sign of courage. Above all it can be seen as a triumph of the human spirit. I see laughter in an African context as a wonderful and enviable trait, one that is exclusively positive in character and one that is present in all Africans, old and young.

If a European child is playing with African children, as sometimes happens, and he starts to cry in a manner that usually denotes that he wants attention, the African children will stop what they are doing and look at him in bewilderment as if an alien has landed in their midst. African children normally associate such behaviour with a grievous mishap like being bitten by a snake or stung by a bee and they are at a loss to understand what is bothering him. A white child crying is a show-stopper and African children will immediately go and look for an adult to take charge of the situation because they sense that it is beyond them.

At the time when her husband was American President, Hilary Clinton made famous the phrase 'in Africa it takes a village to raise a child'. The statement makes good sense so let us take a look at how an African village raises a child.

From the moment a child is born it belongs to the whole village, an example of which is that when growing up he will always refer to his aunts, of whom there will be a great many because African families tend to be big, as his 'mother'. An aunt will have the same authority over a child as the mother; she will show the same concern and affection as the mother and she will also apply the same measure of control. A child's life is filled with authority figures whichever way he looks. Furthermore all the siblings in the village, and not just those of the immediate family, will be referred to as 'brothers' and 'sisters'. It took me a while to grasp this and it was only when I decided to pin an African friend down one day by asking him if the person he had just introduced me to as his 'brother' really was his brother with the same mother and father and he conceded that he was not that the truth finally came out. Mind you, he had to think about it for a second or two before answering which suggested that he was not entirely sure himself.

The implications of extended-family relationships are many and most of them appear extremely onerous by European standards. In fact they can appear onerous by African standards as well, especially in a modern society when one of them happens to move up in the world and gets a job in town with all its attendant financial obligations and a relative descends on him from out of the blue. They would not normally admit to it, however, not even if the demands of the village relationship risked breaking the bank, nor would they ask how long the visitor intends to stay. This does not necessarily mean that they are happy about their visitor dropping in on them unexpectedly – far from it. I have heard enough colleagues and friends complaining about such practices over the years to know that they may dislike it intensely. All the same, tradition usually prevails.

A village member's right to hospitality is normally guaranteed just as it was back in the village where it would be unthinkable for one family to have enough to eat while another goes without. This relationship survives maturity and moving away from the village. A visiting village member can expect the right to a bed and a meal for to refuse would bring shame on the host. Mind you, the guest will be expected to do his share of whatever work needs to be done. The tradition in Tanzania, for example, is that 'on the third day the guest picks up a jembe' – a hoe – and works the land, although more often than not he will get to work the morning after his arrival. Similarly, whenever an errant son or daughter returns to the village he cannot arrive empty handed. He will be expected to come bearing copious gifts for not to do so would again bring shame on his family.

When a village brother or sister needs help, whether in the form of cash, kind or labour, you are expected to respond. Unlike Europe, however, there is no quid pro quo. No-one says 'I am lending you five pounds so you must pay me back this same amount'. It is even possible that the borrower will come back the following week and ask for a second loan before the first one has been repaid, and that he will receive it. And there is every likelihood that he has no intention of ever paying the money back at all and this is not because he is irresponsible or dishonest, nor that he is not sincerely grateful for the help that is being given, it simply means that he is not able to pay the money back, at least not in cash, and the lender will understand this.

It all sounds a bit one-sided but the system works like this: although the families in the village are responsible for their own food production there is a higher principle involved which recognises that should anyone fall upon hard times the others are there to help. In this manner the responsibility for survival is a collective one that is shared by all the village members. Written into this implicit arrangement, albeit in invisible ink, is the knowledge that if the situation is ever reversed so that the one who is helping now should ever need assistance he can call in the favour and expect to be reimbursed in full, no questions asked. It is the African village equivalent of our social security system.

This is all well and good within an African context but one might imagine the reaction of a European who may not understand the rules of the game too well, nor the daily pain of an African's struggle to survive, and thinks that he has been most generous in handing over five pounds only to see his African friend come back the following week and ask for another five pounds. The chances are that the African will be given short shrift and he may not understand why. I know because it has happened to me on a number of occasions and this was my reaction, at least at first. Nowadays I tend to meet my borrower half way and try to explain to him that we do things a bit differently back home and that the money will need to be repaid at some point. I see it as an exercise in furthering international relations which seldom works, of course, not least because many Africans have now cottoned onto the fact that most Europeans will be heading off into the sunset at some point and with any luck they will take their invisible IOU with them.

The transaction is made the more difficult from a European perspective because an African may not expect to have to say 'thank you' for this act of kindness. Back in the village it is everyone's bounden duty to help everyone else and so the expression of gratitude becomes redundant. In fact to say 'thank you' would be tantamount to insulting a brother or sister by saying 'what is the matter with you, you are actually helping someone else for once!' The European, as you can probably imagine, who has been trained from his earliest days to say 'thank you' profusely for just about everything he gets, does not interpret the omission in quite the same way and is likely to interpret it as ingratitude. On such flimsy foundations of missed cues is prejudice often built.

There are other important aspects to village parenting. The moment a child steps out of his hut he is surrounded by peers so there is never any shortage of playmates. They will all move freely in and out of each other's homes so there is no demarcation between families and no geographical limits. The aunt and the uncle have the authority of the parent to control and discipline the child if they feel he needs it and no-one will complain if they do.

There will always be an adult on hand to keep an eye on them while they are playing.

There will be few toys to play with apart from the odd rag doll or the device that fathers sometimes put together - the piece of wire with a metal hoop attached to one end that the children roll along the ground, a bit like a grounds-man might do when marking out a football pitch. Whatever toys exist belong to all the children and there is little sense of individual ownership. A child is unlikely to go running to his mother to complain if a brother or sister takes his toy from him. Incidentally, there is minimal theft in villages. Since property tends to be communal and therefore belongs to everyone there would be little point in stealing from oneself. Neither could it be concealed if such a thing were to happen.

Discipline is strict and children are not allowed to answer back. It is a sure bet that the discipline of the school is an extension of the discipline of the home and that the authority of the teacher is the same authority enjoyed by an aunt or uncle. Crying is practically a taboo. Children learn to tolerate pain because pain, as Africans see it, is an inescapable part of life and the sooner this is learnt the better, recognising no doubt that a plant when it is young and tender can be trained more easily than when it is set in its way.

There is a different attitude towards suffering generally in Africa and I myself have come to see wisdom in it. Most of us in Europe abhor the thought of suffering in any shape or form and no more so than when a child is involved. To see young children caught up in civil conflict, for example, as we sometimes see in news reports is heart-rending and rebels against everything that we have been taught to believe is right and proper. Nonetheless my own perception is that children are under a special protection when it comes to suffering of this kind and that it is the parents who suffer most on their behalf.

I have often wondered why greater effort is not made by television news channels to convey a more realistic picture of the atrocities that are taking place in different parts of the world. Not only do I believe that people have a right to know what is going on, I believe that they *ought* to know. I am certainly not suggesting that we should enter into gory detail but at least let us move beyond the customary 'we warn you that some of the following images may be graphic' which rarely tells us very much and learn what is actually happening. If thousands of men, women and children in Sierra Leone have had limbs violently amputated, for example, then the people of Britain should know about it. There seems to be something of a taboo about accurately reporting such events and I suspect that a reluctance to subject our children to such experiences, even vicariously through the medium of television, may be at the heart of it.

This subject might be worth looking into because my suspicion is that children may well be able to handle atrocities of this kind better than adults think, and possibly even better than adults themselves. Of course they might come up with questions that adults find difficult to answer like, 'Daddy why don't you stop it?' But even this can be beneficial if it leads to a fuller appreciation of what some people have to bear and others do not. Too much security can be a bad thing if it leads to selfishness and arrogance. I am not convinced that it is wise to shield children from what is going on in the world in this fashion. We may be depriving them of an opportunity to learn an important lesson about suffering and to develop a sense of compassion early on in their lives.

There is one aspect of a child's life in the village that strikes me as being particularly beneficial and that is the omnipresence of hardship. It is my personal belief that hardship is therapeutic for the human condition generally and the sooner we accustom ourselves to it the better. Rather than shielding our children from hardship we should be actively introducing them to it from an early age. Needless to say I am talking only of hardship and nothing that could possibly be termed 'exploitation' or 'abuse' – heaven forbid! Africans give their children real jobs of work to do with real responsibility as soon as they are old enough, be it caring for siblings, sweeping the hut and its surrounds, tending small animals or fetching water from the well. How often have I seen the face of a young boy or girl, perhaps seven or eight years old, fixed with concentration as they struggle to get back from a trip to the hand pump with a bucket of water steadied with both hands balanced delicately on their heads, desperately trying not to spill a drop, and with such pride of accomplishment when they manage it!

Everywhere in my travels I have seen how children love to help their parents in their work - the little girl who sits patiently by the side of her mother's stall in the market, or the little boy who accompanies his driver-father on a journey or helps him in the field at planting and harvest time. Humanitarian organisations are often quick to cry 'child labour!' at the first sign of a child engaged in any kind of work activity when in fact there may be nothing wrong with it. We are not talking here about the sweat shops of Asia; what we are talking about is a child accompanying a parent on his daily round and contributing just a modest amount of effort, the result of which makes him feel worthy and needed while at the same time teaching him that work is a necessary part of life.

We might consider, too, the effect that growing up as one of a large number of siblings, some of whom will die, can have on our sense of self-worth. It is unlikely that someone emerging from such a background would consider himself to be the centre of the universe. The Australian writer and critic, Clive James, once humorously remarked that 'History is that series of events leading up to me'. I suspect that not too many Africans would see the joke.

There is, however, one aspect of African parenting that I find myself perpetually at odds with and that is the literal interpretation of 'spare the rod and spoil the child'. If hardship is present in sufficient measure, which it always is, then corporal punishment should not, in my view, be necessary. In fact corporal punishment is a common fact of life in Africa and a harsh one at that. One soon notes that the word 'beat' crops up in conversation with disturbing frequency. I cannot help feeling, although I suspect that most Africans would deny it – in perhaps the way that some adults in Britain are fond of saying that 'a good hiding never did me any harm!' - that a sound beating leaves a child smarting on the inside and with an inner reservoir of pain that may one day vent itself on someone else.

Our visit to the African village would not be complete without mention of the ancient and wonderful art of story-telling which is at the heart of village life. It is a privilege to be present when all the members from the very old to the very young gather around a wood fire in the evening, their faces lit by a brilliant moon and the flicker of the flames, to listen to a storyteller. An elder will recount tales in the local language, tales that seem to go on forever, tales of the past, magical tales, impossible tales, tales that keep everyone enthralled even though most will have heard them many times before. Originality is not a requirement for such occasions. The children become transfixed by these tales, hanging on the story-teller's every word, laughing, sighing, groaning, gasping in turn, their faces a picture of concentration.

Then come the singing and dancing with every single person springing to his feet at the first touch of a drum. No-one is left out; it is a perfect circle that leaves no-one unembraced. A meeting of virtually any description in Africa - church meetings, sports meetings, political meetings - in fact gatherings of any kind would be incomplete without singing and dancing. What has always impressed me most is the seamless transition from daily living to dancing, the one leading to the other so effortlessly and imperceptibly that you hardly notice it taking place. I recall once seeing a policewoman on traffic duty in the town of Wau in South Sudan. There were no vehicles in sight and there she was in the middle of the road perfectly alone and dancing, quite oblivious as to who might be watching. I imagined that she was just feeling happy, gloriously, unselfconsciously happy, and when you feel like this the only thing you can do is dance!

Finally, there is the belief in an after-life and the spirits who have gone before who are always on hand to accompany and help those who are on this earthly plane. There is no clear separation of worlds and the one interacts continuously with the other. Christianity is of course to be seen in strength everywhere and shows no signs of waning but its presence has not entirely cancelled out traditional beliefs. In any case I am not entirely sure that there is a contradiction between the two given that some branches of Christianity recognise the capacity of holy souls like the saints to intercede on our earthly behalf. I myself have little doubt that my mechanic father has helped me solve problems a number of times when my Land Rover has broken down in the middle of nowhere. Still, this is a debate for another occasion. For the moment let us recognise that a good many Africans live in awe of their ancestors who are as real to them as you and me. Death is not the Great Unknown for them that it is for Europeans and I suspect that the transition from one state of being to the other may well be as seamless for an African villager as the one from the magic of the story-teller to the spell of the drum.

The forgoing is intended to provide a brief impression of what life in an Africa village is like and why a child who lives there may not feel a sense of insecurity or want even though by European standards he may lack most of the things that are considered necessary for a contented life. Where does all of this leave African children? If we take as our starting point the recognition that the love of a parent for a child is universal, which is what I have found to be the case everywhere I have been, then I believe it leaves them like this:

i) With boundaries and a structure to their lives;

ii) With a sense of belonging to, and of responsibility towards, a community that is bigger and more important than they are;

iii) With respect for their elders;

iv) With a sense of security and a feeling of being needed;

v) With an ability to see a task once undertaken through to its completion;

vi) With no feelings of self-pity;

vii) With instincts that are selfless and undemanding, and considerate of the needs of others;

viii) With a tolerance for pain;

ix) With a sense of gratitude for who they are and for what they have;

x) With faces radiant and wreathed in smiles;

xi) With courage and enthusiasm;

xii) With an independence of spirit that derives from being given genuine responsibility;

xiii) With the ability to see through their own eyes and not through the eyes of others;

xiv) With an acceptance of death.

Coincidentally, while I was writing this chapter in the house of a friend in Nairobi I happened to see an interview on national television with a British psychologist named Dr. Chris Hart who is based in Nairobi and who seemed to be profoundly knowledgeable of both British and African cultures. I made a few notes of what he had to say which I will share with you now. I missed the first part of the interview and so I do not know if his comments were in response to the deep concerns that many Kenyans feel about the direction that their society is taking in our modern world, but what I can say with confidence is that he certainly gained the full attention of the Kenyan woman who was conducting the interview.

- Children can be tyrants; if they suspect that they can get what they want they will kill you!

- If you do not learn to differentiate between a child's wants and a child's needs, they will run you ragged;

- Children need boundaries;

- They like chores;

- They like structure;

- They like consistency;

- They like to know that if they break the rules 'X' will happen;

- Be firm with them;

- Hardship is a good medium of instruction;

- Little girls can learn early on that they can control their parents;

- If they learn that homework comes first they are learning to make good choices;

- If you are permissive you are storing up lots of trouble for them; they may turn to drugs.

I will leave you with these few comments of Dr. Chris Hart while suggesting that you might want to track him down via the internet to read what else he has to say, something that I will do myself when I have a free moment. I personally found the interview, which was an hour in length, extremely interesting. The subject is clearly of great importance.

Nursery school children stand up to greet visitors, Kiziba refugee camp, Rwanda.

Primary school children, Kiziba refugee camp, Rwanda

A classroom in the primary school, Kiziba refugee camp, Rwanda

Young kids pose for a photograph, Kiziba refugee camp, Rwanda

Young Congolese girls returning from a trip to the bush to collect firewood,
Kiziba refugee camp, Rwanda

A refugee boy transporting firewood on homemade scooter,
equipped with suspension and rear brake, Kiziba refugee camp, Rwanda

Section 2

WHAT ARE WE DEALING WITH?

Chapter Five

DEFINING OUR TERMS

Everything suggests that we are not going to get very far in our search for an answer to life's most pressing problems if we do not define our terms and the first one that needs to be defined is the word 'spiritual'. This chapter is dedicated to such an endeavour while acknowledging from the outset that words in themselves can only ever point in a certain direction, they cannot take us to our destination. An experience is something that has to be *lived*. It is not a thought or an idea or a theory that can be communicated by words alone. This does not mean that a spiritual experience is any the less valid for its lack of a clear definition; quite the reverse in fact, because spiritual experience constitutes our ultimate reality and as such it occupies a position of pre-eminence in all things human.

The reader will note that the terms 'spirituality' and 'morality' are sometimes used interchangeably in this book and this is permissible where there is overlap between the two. I see morality as being spirituality at the social level or how we apply spirituality in our daily lives. Spirituality is the origin of morality and comes first; morality is an expression of it.

It is a curious thing when I reflect upon it now that so many of us in this time of uncertainty should be willing to consider the Big Bang Theory as if it were gospel when in reality it is no more than what it says, a 'theory', one that might easily be replaced by a new one next week. It may relate to something that Malcolm Muggeridge said in his later years after his conversion to Christianity, that 'the average Westerner has a susceptibility to scientific jargon that would be the envy of an African witchdoctor'. I dearly hope that this is not the case here for what is needed is an open and objective mind. I suspect not, given that the world's situation has changed radically since Malcolm Muggeridge was with us, although to his great credit he did clearly predict the collapse of Western Civilisation, a stance that attracted no small amount of ridicule at the time.

Our current economic and environmental crises have changed all this in the blinking of an eye and we could do worse than to go back and take a second look at some of Mr. Muggeridge's later works. Right now Western Civilisation, along with the rest of the world, is poised on the edge of a yawning chasm and when one is so poised one does not normally pay too much attention to theory, scientific or otherwise, one looks for something solid to hang onto. It is the intention of this book to provide that 'something solid to hang onto'. The Big Bang Theory may have to take a back seat for a while.

When I first began writing this book I promised myself that I would do my best to be brutally honest when relating my own experiences and to lay all my cards on the table whatever the consequences. Our present situation is too delicately poised and the consequences of failure too dire to do otherwise. I want to be fully transparent also because I happen to be very fond of my fellow British citizens and I would like to share this information with them in the hope that they may benefit from the lessons that I myself have learned. To be anything other than fully open and sincere would be to sell them short. At the same time I am only too aware that some of the things I have to say may not be to everyone's liking and may even provoke hostility. Nevertheless I have decided to go ahead. And so without further ado I will get started and I will begin with an autobiographical note so that you might know where I am coming from.

I am grateful for my upbringing, humble though it may have appeared from the outside. I grew up on a prefab estate on the outskirts of Bristol and my father and mother were shop assistants at the local Co-op. Later on they progressed to become a factory safety officer and a hospital administrator respectively. Now, with the hindsight of having worked for thirty years in developing countries, I can see that what may have been considered lowly by UK standards put me in the top ten percent of humanity. To always have more than enough to eat, something decent to wear, to have a detached bungalow to live in with a garden front and back, running water (hot and cold), a constant electricity supply, a very good primary school just two hundred yards away, Dr. H. Leader O'Sullivan just down the road whom we could consult free of charge and a hospital close by in case of need - all these were privileges that I only came to appreciate later on in life. And to these we may add an honest and incorruptible police force and a public administration that always did its best to be competent and fair. They say 'travel broadens the mind' and it certainly has in my case. It has given me a wider perspective and an appreciation of what the United Kingdom has provided for its citizens and for which I believe we should all be eternally grateful.

Like most people on the prefab estate, my parents were honest, decent folk who had an innate respect for the values of Christianity but never went to church apart from weddings and funerals. There was a church on the estate – St. Giles – but its presence along with its peripatetic vicar were largely ignored by the residents and it was soon put to other non-religious uses, most notably an additional classroom for an expanding primary school, a place where the boy scouts and girl guides could hold their meetings, and occasionally a cinema. In retrospect I can now see that we were blessed by the values that prevailed on the estate in those days which, although no longer the product of daily worship were still the legacy of a once vibrant Christianity and provided stability and direction. During these years, 1947-1964, there was no crime on the estate to speak of. Such things as burglary, vandalism, gangs, alcoholism, wife-beating, divorce and even bad language in public were virtually unknown. And of course there were no drugs beyond those prescribed by Dr. O'Sullivan.

I need to return to St. Giles for a brief moment because I realise now as I write this that Sunday school must have continued for some good while since I clearly recall attending classes over a period of several weeks when I was probably about twelve years old and I found myself actually enjoying it. I soon yielded, however, to the persuasion of friends who felt that my time could be better spent in other pursuits. And thus began my journey into a spiritual wilderness that lasted for about twenty years.

And a wilderness it truly was. It was a terrible time in which I searched in vain for an identity and wandered aimlessly around in a permanent state of fear, a genuinely lost soul who lacked the courage to admit as much even to himself. I read somewhere that 'there is no oppression greater than to long for the truth and not know where to find it' and this summed up my position perfectly. My existence was one of quiet despair into which the light of day never entered, a living nightmare that left me alienated from the world and longing for release at every moment. Small wonder that I eventually went to university to study literature where the notion of life as absurd had taken hold. To know that I was not alone may have helped but it did not provide the answers that I needed.

I had a premonition of my change of fortune in a dream when I was twenty-nine years old, about six months before I moved to Liverpool to study for a Masters degree in Latin American politics. In the dream I was lying face-down in a cave in total darkness barely able to move. Then a light appeared at the mouth of the cave like the gentle light of dawn and it was only this that allowed me to see the full extent of my captivity. Next I found myself outside the cave walking through a sunlit wood with two kindly soldiers protecting me, one on either side. The following night the same dream continued and this time I found myself playing rugby – a game that I was never very good at – where I easily evaded the tackles of my opponents and basked in the glory of triumphant victory.

It was in Liverpool in November 1974 that I had my first spiritual experience and it was also in Liverpool in July 1975, in the same room where I was living as a student, that I had my second. Both experiences changed my life profoundly and forever and I will tell you about them in a later chapter. At first I thought the location was incidental but I have since wondered about Liverpool. I recall reading somewhere, possibly in Memories, Dreams and Reflections by Carl Jung, that Liverpool was considered at one time to be a place of pilgrimage. The seat of the soul in those ancient days was believed to be the liver rather than the heart, and the pool relates to the pool of life – spiritual life. It certainly is a vibrant city as anyone who has lived there will know.

It is not always easy nowadays to understand what is being implied when the term 'spiritual' is used because so much religious metaphor has been borrowed by the world of popular culture that the lines between the two have become blurred. We hear pop songs that speak of 'The Glory of Love', and being 'Born Again', and John Lennon told us that 'the way things are going they're gonna crucify me'. There has been a certain amount of cross-over as the writers of popular songs have sought ever more creative ways to impress us with their depth of feeling. It has always been understood even by agnostics that religious experience with its associations of martyrdom and sacrifice represents the ultimate expression of human commitment and so it should not be surprising if its terminology is borrowed by others, even if their motivation is less selfless.

The word 'spiritual' has been abused right across the board in our modern society as we instinctively seek to share with others the importance of our life's discoveries to the point that it has lost much of its original meaning. We hear such things as, 'sex is a spiritual experience', or 'climbing a mountain is a spiritual experience', or even 'eating organic food is a spiritual experience'. In fact none of this is true, nor is it even possible.

My own belief, and it is drawn from personal experience as described in Chapter Seven, is that a spiritual experience is by definition non-material which means that it cannot be induced by material means. A spiritual experience will be non-material from start to finish. It cannot be induced, for example, by marihuana, cocaine, opium, ayahuasca or peyote. Such experiences as follow the ingestion of physical substances are the result of chemical changes that take place in the body and can in no way be considered to be spiritual. And this, of course, is how it should be and can only be if the higher self, as explained in Chapter Three, is 'associated with the body but not part of it' and is 'the eternal part of us that survives the decomposition of the body'.

It is clear that certain types of music, literature and art, if it is spiritually inspired, can lift us to greater heights and point us in the right direction, and we should be thankful for it and know that we can turn to it for inspiration whenever we need it, but its effect can only ever be temporary.

Notwithstanding a direct intervention in our lives by the Creator of the kind that Paul experienced on the road to Damascus, the only experiences that may said to be able to effect permanent change in our spiritual condition are prayer, meditation, the study of holy texts and service in a holy cause. Of these it is prayer with its immediately accessible power to transform our persons and our situations that is pre-eminent. Prayer is exceedingly simple although it is not always easy to perform and this is because it demands humility on two accounts: the first is because it recognises the existence of a conscious force that is greater than ourselves and whose assistance we must actively seek; and the second is because it involves the surrender of the ego which is none other than the lower self with all its crowding appetites that we heard of earlier. Neither is prayer the result of any intellectual effort. Rather it represents an effort of will and as such it turns life into a level playing field because through it the door of true understanding is opened to everyone regardless of their level of intelligence or their educational background.

The great myth and Achilles heel of our modern world is the belief that truth is exclusively accessible through the intellect. This is a false and a dangerous assumption. The intellect is useful for a great many things, like producing technology, for example, which has made life infinitely more bearable and entertaining, but insight of the kind that leads to an understanding of the meaning of life is not the prerogative of intellectuals, someone who happens to have a doctorate in biology or physics, but of every single person who is alive, because anyone, regardless of his intelligence quota is capable of summoning up the will to engage in prayer. The only thing that stands in the way is ego, nothing else, and so it must be if, as promised, the meek are to inherit the earth.

Chapter Six

CHRISTIANITY TODAY

One of the abiding memories of my arrival in Ecuador in 1968 as a young volunteer was opening a newspaper and seeing the photograph of a pathetic-looking young man behind bars. The caption read 'Sentenced for his brother's crime'. The article told how the police had been unable to catch the man they were looking for and so they arrested his brother instead.

Everything inside me rebelled against the injustice of such an act and I instantly started to wonder what sort of country I had volunteered to serve in. Such a thing could not possibly happen back in England, I told myself, and thankfully I was right, it could not. It was my first lesson in adapting to a foreign culture and it was a good one because it helped me to understand what justice was all about and how important it is both for the individual and for society whose stability depends upon it. I later learned that this was a curious aberration in Ecuador's legal system, which was presumably why the article appeared in the newspaper, and that Ecuador's record in human rights is really quite good, especially by Latin American standards. I often reply to people when they ask me what Ecuador is like by saying that it is an oasis of sanity between two crazy neighbours, meaning Peru and Colombia, the latter quite often being referred to these days, even by Colombians themselves, as 'Locombia' - the crazy country.

A second incident soon followed where I saw a man lying in the street and no-one was stopping to help him; in fact they walked right past him as if he were not there. Again I sought consolation by telling myself that this could not happen back home and in those days, the late nineteen sixties, it could not. If we did actually see someone lying helplessly on the street, which would have been very rare, our first instinct would have been to stop and help. Sadly such things are now a thing of the past because the sight of people lying on our streets has become all too common. No doubt there are a number of reasons for it but presumably the liberalisation of the sale of alcohol, the relentless advertising that promotes it and the proliferation of hard drugs, something that was unthinkable in the nineteen sixties, must have something to do with it.

The image of the wretch behind bars somehow stayed with me and I had reason to think back to it some years later when I started to take an interest in spiritual matters and began to investigate the world's religions. Like most people in Britain I had grown up in a Christian tradition attending first a primary school and then a secondary school where prayers were said every morning and where religious instruction was the only compulsory subject on the curriculum even if there was no examination at the end of the year. I had not taken too much interest in religion at the time but somewhere inside me I recognised that Christianity represented a definite truth and told myself that if I were ever to take up a religion seriously then Christianity would probably be the one.

A major stumbling block I had was the notion of original sin. It seemed to me grossly unfair that a whole race of people should be punished for something that Adam supposedly did back in the distant mists of time. Furthermore, if this guilt was cast over everyone until the time that Jesus Christ reputedly came as a sacrifice for Adam's sin to liberate us from our past, then it also covered the likes of holy men such as Abraham, Moses and the Jewish prophets. It was all too much for my feeble brain to handle and so I did what most people do in such circumstances, I shelved it for another day. Who was I, after all, to challenge notions that infinitely more capable minds than mine had been able to accept?

As the years went by and my knowledge of religion increased, as did my confidence along with it, I realised that my early misgivings had been well founded and that the notion of Adam's sin being cast over someone else, even one person let alone the whole human race, was indeed unreasonable. Or, if it really was the case, then the God of the Bible was not a kindly old man after all but a despot. This realisation was compounded by the line in Chapter 14 verse 6 of John's Gospel that evangelical Christians are fond of quoting, 'I am the way the truth and the life. No one comes to the Father except through me'. Here again I had cause to back off for I had met so many honourable people in different parts of the world, men and women who were decent, responsible, compassionate, law-abiding citizens who were not Christians and who, therefore, according to the evangelists, were going to spend eternity 'burning in the lake fires of hell' for not accepting Jesus Christ 'as their personal saviour'. Once again my sense of fair play rebelled and a voice inside me said 'anyone who treats good and honest people like this cannot be a just and loving God'. Indeed, not even the worst of the Roman emperors had treated their subjects in such a capricious and cruel fashion.

I recall watching the world-renowned healing evangelist, Benny Hinn, who appears regularly on Trinity Broadcast Network, the Christian TV channel that broadcasts around the world and around the clock out of California, preaching to a massed crowd in India. There must have been over a million people present in the open air arena on this particular occasion which would have made it one of the biggest voluntary gatherings in history. This in itself should have made it worthy of mention in the international press but for some reason it was not.

Benny Hinn is a remarkable man who has been spectacularly healing very sick people by non-material means in full public view for over thirty years. This too should have caught the attention of the world's press but it seldom has. More often the news industry has focussed its efforts on trying to expose him as a fraud which it has not been able to do. If we pause to think about this, that not a single person in thirty years has come forward to confess to having faked a recovery and yet the media still refuses to acknowledge the remarkable healing power that is present in Benny Hinn's meetings, it says much about the bias of the news industry today. As I say this I can already hear the sound of knives sharpening and so I will leave the matter where it is. I have no wish to increase Benny Hinn's anguish by adding to his number of detractors.

At the end of his meetings Benny Hinn, in keeping with most TV evangelists, invites the audience, both those present and those watching by television, to give their lives to Christ. What brought home to me the full agony of the Christian dilemma inherent in their message of 'either accept Christ as your personal saviour or spend eternity burning in the lake fires of hell', was a little girl who came forward to the platform on which Benny Hinn was standing in a flood of tears. Benny Hinn in a most kind and fatherly manner asked what was upsetting her and the little girl explained that although she was now a Christian and would be going to heaven her parents were still Hindus and would therefore be going to hell. Benny Hinn put his arm around her and lovingly assured her that 'Christ loves her parents also' which is no doubt true. But then one is again left with the awkward question of 'what sort of God is this that loves you but still consigns you to spend eternity burning in the lake fires of hell?'

The end result was that I abandoned my search for a home in the Christian Church and looked elsewhere for an answer to my own and the world's problems. Since then I, along with a multitude of others, have watched as our churches have emptied and our church leaders have been increasingly relegated to the sidelines. Precious few of our citizens turn to the Anglican Church nowadays for guidance; it is as if they have given up hope of finding anything of value there.

We need to try to understand why this should be for a number of reasons, not least because our church leaders are in the main highly educated, well-intentioned, decent people who have dedicated their lives to serving the members of the British public and have nothing but their best interests at heart. It grieves me to see them disregarded in this fashion. Let us take a step back for a moment and consider Christianity from a historical perspective that includes other faiths as well to see how Christianity compares. The standpoint I take is that of someone who has spent over thirty years investigating religious truth wherever it is to be found.

There are always two aspects to any religion, the *spiritual* which constitutes the core of personal belief and the *social* which deals with relationships. The *spiritual* aspect which is to be found in identical form in all of the world's religions never changes and in this sense may be said to be absolute. It teaches the same message of love, compassion, kindness, generosity, honesty, responsibility, trustworthiness, justice and so forth and constitutes the source of the virtues that we have always been encouraged to aspire to, and herein lies the essential goodness of religion. The *social* aspect, however, is not absolute but relative and evolves according to humanity's needs, which is not surprising when one considers the amazing journey that we have made, as explained in Chapter Two, from the family through the clan, the tribe, the city-state and the nation state to our emerging world community.

Abraham, for example, brought one set of laws; Moses brought another that was based upon the Ten Commandments; Christ brought another which included changing the law of divorce and the law of the Sabbath and no longer demanded 'an eye for an eye' and 'a tooth for a tooth'; and Prophet Mohammed brought yet another set of laws, one that was more elaborate and rigid in character. It will be seen that each of these men of God confirmed the divine mission of his predecessor and introduced new laws that were in keeping with the requirements of society at a particular time. When asked by a follower why he, Christ, forbade divorce whereas his predecessor, Moses, allowed it, Christ explained that the people were too hard-hearted to receive it at that time, thereby providing an example of how our needs evolve in accordance with those of a changing society.

The spiritual core of Christianity is just as relevant to the individual's needs today as it was two thousand years ago and about this there can be no doubt. The social dimension of Christianity, however, which was perfectly adequate for its time, has little to offer a world that is struggling to organise itself along global lines. We are now left having to decide for ourselves whether Christ would have approved or disapproved of such contentious issues as stock markets, banks, personal fortunes, abortion, gay marriage, polygamy, heart transplants, euthanasia, cremation, and so forth. What is needed now is a new set of guidelines that addresses the important issues of our time, one that is global in its embrace and accommodates the needs of an emerging world community with its indissoluble connectedness and its myriad complexity. At the same time it must retain at its core traditional Christian values which, as stated above, happen to be values that are shared by all the world's religions.

Britain appears to be going through a phase right now where it thinks it can survive without religion, many people believing that not only is religion unnecessary but that it actually serves as an impediment to social harmony and progress. The opposite is true in fact, although it may take us a while to see it, just as it did in the last century when we stumbled from one crisis to the next at enormous cost until we finally learned that man-made belief systems – all the 'isms', like Marxism, communism, fascism, nationalism, materialism, racism, humanism and so forth – are flawed and ultimately unworkable. The great lesson of our present century is likely to be that society without religion cannot survive and we will see people returning en masse to lives of prayer and worship, albeit when they have run out of other options.

I must confess that a part of me is glad that the Church of England, defunct though it nearly is, has chosen to disassociate itself from the evangelical movement of the United States with its inflammatory rhetoric and its uncompromising message of salvation. If you happen to watch Trinity Broadcast Network and see the more zealous of its preachers pacing to and fro like caged lions, their voices ever more strident as they call upon Christ to 'wash away their sins with his precious blood' and to return 'on the clouds of heaven' so that 'the dead in Christ can rise up from their graves and meet him in the air', I will be surprised if you do not feel a similar sense of relief.

The United States is a curious country with all its glaring anomalies which, like human foibles everywhere, are no doubt more visible from the outside than from within. How can such a Christian country be so addicted to money? How can such a Christian country be so addicted to sex? How can such a Christian country be so addicted to fame and glamour? How can such a Christian country be so addicted to violence? How can such a Christian country be so accepting of the brutality of capitalism? How can such a Christian country be so afraid of death?

We British often fail to note that although the language is English the culture is not. Many Brits still look upon American culture as an extension of their own, as some sort of distant cousin who has gone out into the world and 'made it big' but who still has roots back in the home country, the way that Australians and New Zealanders do. American culture, however, is a culture all of its own and the ruthless pursuit of its goals makes it, if anything, more Germanic than British. It might be a subject of a doctoral thesis to determine where the dominant cultural traits come from for it is certainly not the British Isles. In escaping from one form of extremism, which no longer exists in the countries they left behind, if indeed it ever really did, they seem to have invented another.

I pity President Obama who, unlike other US Presidents, has travelled the world and learned to appreciate what other countries have to offer and is now saddled with the task of having to enlighten his fellow countrymen. No wonder so many of them hate him! Like Gorbachev he runs the risk of being more popular overseas than at home. And like Gorbachev he may well end up presiding over his nation's demise. No culture can make a virtue of greed and expect to last for very long, although Americans have done a pretty good job of convincing the rest of the world that it can and that others should follow suit. Perhaps the best example of our myopic ambition is to be found in our use of fossil fuels, not only have we contaminated the air we breathe, we have taken a miraculous resource that it took nature two hundred million years to produce and we have used it up in little over a hundred years. It may not prove to be the smartest thing we have ever done.

Nonetheless what does profoundly disturb me about Britain is the absence of any voice of moral authority which is something that cannot be said of the United States where its many churches are loud and clear on a wide range of issues. It is my understanding that the head of the Church of England, the Archbishop of Canterbury, should be the one to take on this role but he has not done so. When, for example, was the last time we heard him speak out against the use of drugs, sexual laxity, abortion, vandalism, gang culture, crime, binge-drinking, domestic violence, the use of obscenities in the media, in fact anything that by its very nature runs counter to the teachings of the New Testament?

I myself cannot recall a single stand that he has taken on anything beyond a recent criticism of the banking system that was issued jointly with other religious leaders. We desperately need a voice of moral authority at this time to counter the growing tide of unrest that is sweeping through our nation and yet the very person who should be the most vocal remains silent.

But the greatest shortcoming of the Church of England has been its failure to communicate to the nation that there exists an intermediary force that links the Creator to His creation and that this intermediary force is called 'the divine spirit'. The divine spirit brings energy and purpose to our spiritual lives just as the rays of the sun with their light and warmth bring energy and purpose to our physical lives and without which all living things will die. This is the principle on which all religion is based and it is also the bedrock on which every civilisation that has ever existed has stood and without which will crumble; and it is why Britain is falling apart right now. It is the divine spirit that holds society together; it alone can enable the higher self to win its battle over the lower self and ensure stability. Its absence is the cause of our recent riots and why they are destined to return with even greater force in the near future.

Surely no greater charge can be laid at the door of the one who is supposed to be the custodian of our spiritual destiny than to allow the people in his charge to become ignorant of the existence of the divine spirit, the most vital experience available to humankind? One cannot help but wonder if he himself has experienced it because once one has tasted of this miraculous gift he can never be the same again, nor can he remain silent about it. Before such irresistible proof all the arguments of all the atheists in the world come to nothing and run like water off a duck's back down the drain. As I write this I estimate that in all probability some ninety percent of our population today have no clear idea of what I am talking about and herein lies the problem.

This is all the evidence we need. The man at the top should be politely encouraged to either speak up or step down, one or the other, his silence is no longer tenable.

Since writing these words the Archbishop of Canterbury has resigned from his post and stepped down. We must now hope that his successor will have the presence of mind to tackle head-on the primary issue of our time, namely, the rapidly deteriorating moral condition of our nation.

Chapter Seven

THE POOL OF LIFE

I had given up all hope of ever finding an answer to my deplorable state. Worse still, I don't think it had even occurred to me that there might be an answer to find. I was probably doing what my parents had done before me which was to keep soldiering on with no expectation that life would or could ever get any better. It was all about survival, nothing more.

I was sitting on the sofa when it happened. It was around seven o'clock in the evening in the middle of November 1974. I do not recall the exact day. I was facing out towards the park which my room with its large bay window overlooked. It was a fine Victorian house with a commanding view built in Liverpool's more prosperous days although it was dark by now and I could not really see beyond the dim lights that lined the paths. I did not have much on my mind at the time. My course work was in hand and it was time for switching off. From out of nowhere came the thought 'Why don't you surrender?' Wherever the thought came from, and to this day I do not know, it interrupted whatever I might have been thinking about and arrested my immediate attention. Instinctively I did what the thought suggested and I surrendered, although I knew not to whom, what, how or why.

For a split second I felt myself being drawn upwards and then my whole being was swamped from head to foot in a torrent of golden light. It was as if a great waterfall had descended upon me charging every atom of my being with energy. It was wonderful, miraculous, exhilarating, ecstatic, comforting, confirming and completely life-changing all at once! It was everything I had ever longed for without even knowing that it was there! Here at last was a reason to live and to go on living, only this time with joy and happiness! In a trice I understood that life was no longer just about survival and playing safe, it was about taking chances, about evading tackles, scoring tries and winning! For the first time in my life I felt truly glad that I was alive! Nothing I had ever experienced could even begin to compare, not even remotely, with the matchless beauty of that moment which filled to overflowing the very essence of my being. The immediate sensation probably only lasted for a couple of seconds although an exquisite tingling sensation stayed with me for several days afterwards. It was all I could do to remain conscious, which I somehow managed to do although not through any effort of my own.

'My God!' I exclaimed, 'Is this what religion is all about?' No wonder it has caused so much upheaval down the ages! I knew instinctively that the experience was legitimate and that I had been filled with the divine spirit. No wonder so many simple, lowly, ungifted men and women, people just like myself, had suddenly been able to turn their lives around and make undreamed-of sacrifices in the service of others! So this was how cowards had become heroes, how gnats had become eagles, how drops of water had become surging oceans, how specks of dust had become scintillating stars, how the disciple Peter who denied Christ three times and ran when the enemy appeared had become a spiritual giant who caused even mighty Rome to quake!

It was the 'Amazing Grace' that the hymn speaks of 'that saved a wretch like me', the same that transformed the life of the notorious slaver John Newton after he had fallen on his knees and prayed in the midst of a terrible storm at sea and caused him to dedicate the rest of his days to fighting the very trade that he had once promoted and had made him rich. It was John Newton who composed the hymn *Amazing Grace* in gratitude for his survival and his salvation, the same man who ended his days dressed in sackcloth and swabbing floors in penance for the wrong that he had done. He had been moved from the pinnacle of success to the depths of nothingness and yet here he found a meaning to his life that moved him like nothing before. All of this suddenly made perfect sense and it came from nowhere!

Then a second thought soon followed – but whatever happened to all this pristine, dynamic, life-changing energy, where did it go? Has it been slowly killed off by clerics and scholars who were never really in touch with the true spirit or, if they were, chose to suppress it out of some puritanical impulse? Somewhere along the line what should have remained a joyful, untrammelled exuberance has become little more than a duty, something to be endured rather than enjoyed. Small wonder that our churches are now empty! Later on I came across a more vibrant form of Christianity in Africa and the Caribbean where the believers have thrown off the shackles of restraint and surrender whole-heartedly to the passion within and when I did I took it as confirmation of the legitimacy of my own discovery.

It quickly dawned on me that the Great Being, whoever he may be, had taken pity on my miserable state and called me to him. My experience, or so I was later told, is what Christians refer to as being 'born again' and there was certainly great similarity with what they describe but there were differences also. For a start there was no expression of will on my part. This is important because Christians usually make the point that in order to 'come to Christ', as they call it, one has to make a choice to do so. I did not make such a choice and in so far as this is the case I have to acknowledge that the Creator, for whatever reason, must have decided to break his own rule of not interfering with our free-will and to impose his own will instead.

This I have interpreted as an indication of the irretrievably hopeless state that I had reached. I did not even have the desire to think about looking for an answer so wretched had I become. I see it now as an act of both generosity and desperation on His part. I can imagine Him saying something like 'What are we going to do with this buffoon?

He really is beyond hope! There is nothing for it, we are going to have to intervene!' It all sounds a bit like the intervention of Clarence in the life of George Bailey in the film *It's a Wonderful Life* when George was about to throw himself off the bridge. It was the same state of hopelessness except that George's awakening was more gradual and less epiphanous than mine. What was it he said to the bizarre-looking Clarence just after he, George, had dragged him from the freezing water and Clarence had told him that he was an angel sent to save his life - 'just my luck to get an angel like you!'

Another important point to note was that I was not in a state of prayer when it happened. In fact if I am to be honest I have to admit that up unto this point, which was just shy of my thirtieth birthday, I had never said a prayer in earnest in my life. So there was really no reason to connect the experience with Christianity at all. Nonetheless I did and it was probably for the reason that I mentioned in Chapter Six, namely, because somewhere inside me at some point in my youth I recognised that Christianity represented a definite truth and that if I were ever to take up a religion it would most likely be Christianity.

Every Sunday morning for at least two months afterwards I attended a church service hoping to find one that I might join on a permanent basis. I always emerged feeling energised and confident but somehow disappointed and I never actually took the step of joining any one of them, although they all, without exception, went out of their way to make me feel welcome. I am not entirely sure why it was but I suspect that it had something to do with the exclusivity of the Christian position. I always felt uneasy about accepting something that might cut me off from the rest of humanity. Gradually the demands of my studies took over and I turned my attention to these instead so that I effectively suspended my search for the time being.

The second experience which took place in the same room at around 3am in the morning of 14th July 1975 was as unexpected, exhilarating, overwhelming and wondrously fulfilling as the first. As I write this now it seems something of a miracle that I managed to complete my course of studies with so much upheaval going on in my private life. Nonetheless I did, and in fact I duly emerged with my Master's degree in hand having passed all my exams comfortably and having submitted my dissertation well within the deadline.

What I did not mention was that staying in the same house in the next room to me was a young Iranian by the name of Hooman who was studying for a doctorate in parasitology. One Sunday afternoon sometime in December, not long after my life-changing experience which incidentally I chose not to mention to anyone, I invited Hooman in for a cup of tea. He mentioned that he was a follower of a relatively new religion called the Baha'i Faith. I took no interest in his comment, assuming that it was just another of the fads that were still reaching us in droves from the East in that post-Beatles era, but I did ask him, more out of politeness than anything, if he would lend me a book so that I might learn something about it. The book that he lent me was called *The Reality of Man* and it lay by my bedside unopened for the next six months, which will give you some idea of how negligent I was in those days.

The preceding night of 13th July I found that I could not sleep which was unusual for me and I was starting to fret. I had an exam the next day and I had revised for it reasonably well and wanted to get a good night's rest so that I could enter the examination room with a clear head. At about 3am on what was now the morning of 14th July I could stand it no longer and decided to turn on the light, whereupon I saw the book that Hooman had lent me still lying unopened by the side of my bed.

'Oh, it's the book the Iranian fellow gave me', I thought, 'I might as well have a look at it'.

I picked it up and opened it at random and read the line, *'This evening I will speak to you concerning the meaning of sacrifice'*. Instantly I entered a world of paradise that was beautiful beyond description! It was as if I had suddenly stepped into a rose garden filled with the most exquisite fragrances with birds singing all around! For a second time in my life, in this same room in Liverpool, and within the space of just eight months, I had the privilege of knowing what it was to have an authentic spiritual experience and this one was every bit as miraculous and convincing as the first. The book was written by the same Persian philosopher that I quoted in Chapter Three, Abdul Baha. I will say more about Baha'i belief later on in the book but suffice it to say at this point that all the misgivings that I had previously felt about identifying with a religion were instantly dispelled. For the moment I could hardly contain my excitement. I got dressed and went for a walk around the park at the unearthly hour of 3am. For a second time I understood that some invisible hand had, unprompted and unasked, beckoned me to enter Paradise and I had accepted. I also knew that I need never leave if I did not want to. I felt as if I could take on the whole world if need be and that I could achieve anything I set my mind to. My joy and my gratitude were boundless!

A number of lessons have subsequently been drawn from these two experiences and no doubt the learning process will continue. Some have already been addressed in previous chapters like the reasons for the decline of the Church and the essential non-material nature of spiritual experience. I have also learned how to heal by non-material means and have been practicing for over twenty years, although nothing on the scale of Benny Hinn, I hasten to add. We have a long and proud tradition of spiritual healing in this country and it is one that deserves to be fully recognised. The greatest healer of all was a man named Harry Edwards whose healing gift along with the sanctuary that he founded in Shere in Surrey should be a source of national pride. The laying on of hands apart, there is a close relationship between the state of our spiritual health and the state of our physical health that modern science is only now beginning to recognise.

Neither of these two experiences has been repeated in the intervening thirty-seven years, nor do they need to be. Their purpose was to provide the stability, the resolve, the energy and the direction that I needed to embark upon my life's journey and I have since been able to turn my life around and do something useful with it. Above all it has meant that I have been able to be of service to others through my work in the humanitarian field. Incidentally, I applied for and was offered my first job with Voluntary Service Overseas where I spent thirteen of the happiest years of my life, a job that was perfect in every sense and set me on the right path, even before I had completed my studies.

I became a new person during the year in Liverpool, someone who bears scant resemblance to the old one. Of course the old one is still lurking somewhere in the shadows as a constant reminder of the wretch that once was, and he can still cause me to cringe now and again at the thought of some of the things I have said and done but he is no longer the dominant presence that he once was. He has been relegated to the sidelines where he belongs.

It has not been all plain sailing and it would be wrong to imply that it has because obstacles still remain. This is to be expected as part of a learning process that will probably go on forever. I read somewhere that if you ever come across a road without obstacles it probably does not lead anywhere and this sounds about right. The hardest part I have found is to forgive myself for the wrongs I have committed, especially some of the hurtful things that I have said to people who did not hurt me, not even in retaliation, things that were said out of malice. I know that this battle is in large part inside my own head because on the occasions that I have taken the matter in hand and apologised for something that I have said or done, the person concerned usually had only scant recollection of an incident that had been tormenting me for years. There is wisdom in the saying 'never take yourself too seriously; no-one else does'.

As for conquering the lower self – I don't honestly think we can, not completely, at least not while we are on this earth and certainly not by our own efforts. The love of self is kneaded into the human clay. It is better to speak of 'escape' rather than conquest, and a temporary one at that, and the only sure way of escaping is to turn towards the Great Being in prayer on a daily basis and to ask for his assistance. In this fashion we will develop the higher self which always takes place, as we have noted, at the expense of the lower self. It is a slow process and one to be undertaken a single step at a time; and patience is essential.

The conclusion I have reached with regard to conquering the lower self by our own efforts, as some cultures try to do by flagellating themselves or shutting themselves away in monasteries, is that it does not work. It does not work because the one who is calling the shots is also the one who is causing the problem and putting oneself to the test is not the answer. This may sound harsh on those who have chosen a monastic life-style but I favour the view of the poet John Milton who said *'I cannot praise a fugitive and cloistered virtue...that never sallies out and sees her adversary'*. In the end the answer is not to be found in seclusion but in positive engagement with the world around us, and in surrender too, of course – the surrender of our entire being into the hands of One who is infinitely wiser and more able than we are, One whose existence I had never even suspected until that day when He chose to reach down and pluck me from a sea of despair.

I maintain every conceivable sympathy for those who have been crushed by life, who would prefer to stay indoors and never put a foot outside, and even those who turn to alcohol and drugs in a last-ditch effort to survive in what is for them a soulless world. But I also know that in the end such things can never provide an answer. True happiness can never be found in material things – and no, they do not even *help*, so please do not throw this one back at me. And this brings me right back to the child in the African village with nothing who is infinitely happier than the child in Britain with everything.

Without a spiritual foundation to our lives material things will not bring happiness, in fact they are a hindrance. What is being recommended here is not asceticism - sackcloth and ashes - but detachment. There is nothing wrong with material things provided we do not seek happiness in their acquisition. They must never be allowed to obstruct our view of the infinite. If we lie awake at night thinking about the new car that we want to buy, or how we can invest our money for maximum return, or even imagining what Mr. Right will look like when he comes along, the chances are that we will be disappointed. We have first to learn how to become detached and when we do it will not really matter what sort of car we buy. Furthermore there is every likelihood that our cash return will be just what we need and that the butterfly we have been chasing will come and settle on our shoulder. Detachment is something that can be learned and acquired by anyone at any time wherever he happens to be and without changing one iota of his surroundings. The two are not incompatible. In the end it is a question of attitude, do we own what surrounds us or does it own us? If it is the former then we have nothing to lose or fear.

Chapter Eight

CREATIVE FORCES

We have already considered one seriously harmful myth of our time, the myth that truth is exclusively accessible through the intellect. We will now consider a second harmful myth, the myth that society moves forward as a result of the influence of certain gifted individuals, most notably scientists and social reformers – Newton, Wilberforce, Faraday, Lincoln, Einstein, for example - whose insight and perhaps courage also, break new ground and open up a way for the masses to follow, the quality of their lives being greatly improved. The United States is particularly prone to such notions under the heading of 'leadership' which constitutes the organising principle of much of American life. The idea that our progress as a species should ultimately depend on the visionary powers of certain gifted individuals, however, is quite false and constitutes one of the major causes of our present global predicament. Society does not work like this at all.

This chapter intends to show that our fixation with the notion of gifted individuals as problem-solvers has led us into a dead-end and I shall be drawing upon my experiences in the humanitarian field to illustrate the point. We will then move on to consider an alternative view of how humanity progresses. It is a complex issue and I prefer to start with the conclusion and then go back to the argument so that we know exactly where we stand. Clarity here is crucial and I have no wish to lose anyone along the way.

It is essential to understand that the forces that have determined the course of mankind's evolution from its earliest hunter-gatherer days to the complex world that we now live in have all derived from the power that is contained within divine religion. We could take any of the world's religions to illustrate this point but I will take just one, Islam, which we will look at in a moment. I have chosen Islam because it is generally recognised to be the most recent of the world's Faiths and provides the clearest example of the point I wish to make. I have chosen it also because Islam has received an extraordinarily bad press of late and I would like to try to restore a semblance of balance.

The genesis of all major social change is as follows and it is one that has been repeated over and over down the ages. A very special kind of human being appears in our midst, an Abraham, a Krishna, a Moses, a Buddha, a Christ, a Mohammed, one who claims to be a messenger of God whose role it is to educate and guide mankind to new levels of achievement both in terms of their knowledge and the way that they treat each other. Despite the many prophecies surrounding his appearance the messenger of God is invariably rejected by his people, usually because the religious leaders of the time see their authority threatened and declare him to be an imposter. The very ones who should have been the first to recognise him are often the last.

The new message still manages to take hold but through the receptivity of the meek and humble, the supposed lesser mortals in our midst who because of their meekness have the purity of heart needed to recognise the truth of the new message. It takes humility to see it. Despite great opposition that takes the form of scorn, persecution, torture and death, in fact every possible attempt to root out what is seen as heresy, the new religion survives, gains ground and eventually flourishes. The spiritual power that it contains is released into the world through the words that the messenger of God utters and creates a new consciousness which allows for the emergence of a new social order, one that is based on justice and compassion while stimulating new and wonderful advances in the arts and sciences. A golden age of civilisation is ushered in. All the major advances that are witnessed across a wide spectrum of human endeavour are the fruits of this new flowering of consciousness. They are, however, only ever the fruits, they are never the cause.

It follows that gifted individuals, the scientists and the social reformers, are not those who are primarily responsible for society's progress. Rather they themselves are the product of a socio-cultural context which is made up of a critical mass of people whose collective values determine society's potential for advancement. Thus it should be seen that the people who have traditionally been considered as our leaders are in fact the servants of the masses and are dependent upon the masses both for their inspiration and their impact. It is the masses who provide gifted individuals with the opportunity to exercise their talents rather than the gifted individuals who provide the masses with the opportunity to progress. While it is clear that the one necessarily serves the other it is evident that the importance of the socio-cultural context far exceeds that of the gifted individual, not least because the former can exist without the latter whereas the latter cannot exist without the former.

The appearance of scientific inventions in our modern world sheds more light on this relationship. The invention of photography dates back to the mid-eighteenth century with important inputs first from Japan and Germany and then later from France, Britain and America, with principal inventors Hishida, Schultze, Niepce and Daguerre, Talbot and Eastman adding to each other's discoveries within the space of a hundred years. It is clear that what we are witnessing here is a new 'spirit of the age' that affected a great many inventors rather than a single individual who leads the way for others to follow. With television we see a similar thing. If you ask a German, a Frenchman, a Brit, a Russian, a Hungarian or an American who invented television you will probably get six different answers depending on which nationality you happen to be talking to at the time. Here we see again that each of the inventors was dependent for his discovery upon the presence of a supportive culture of scientific enquiry that was emerging simultaneously in different places, albeit with a certain amount of cross fertilization of ideas going on between them. The same could be said of the Wright brothers' first manned flight. If they had not been successful in December 1903 someone else would have succeeded very soon afterwards. The Wright brothers realised a new potential that was made available to all those who belonged to a technology based culture and they happened to get there first. I suspect that the urgency with which they pursued their goal is an indication of their sense that the race was truly on.

I saw this most clearly when I was working in South Sudan which is one of the least developed places on earth. Many of the aid agencies, particularly those from the United States, design their strategies around certain key individuals in the local community whom they refer to as 'champions', meaning people who have been identified as being worthy to be trained and who can thereafter lead the transformation of their communities. In aid circles this is often referred to as 'empowerment'. The only problem is that it does not work, it never has and it never will.

It does not work because society only depends on individuals for its transformation in a secondary sense. A supportive culture must first be in place before change can occur and no significant transfer of technical know-how is possible until it is, no matter how gifted the 'champion' may be. And to assume that someone with the right drive and motivation could ever be capable of inspiring enough people around him as to create a requisite critical mass of supportive culture is an illusion. It cannot be done. What is needed, as a bare minimum - and even then there is no guarantee that it will work - is the 'education, education, education' of large numbers of people over several decades. As the saying goes, 'if you want to educate a man you must start with his grandfather'. In other words, there are no quick fixes to social and economic development and to pretend that there are is dishonest.

Driving this disastrous approach to social and economic development, parallel with an obsession with leadership, is the belief also prominent among Americans that 'anyone can be a winner' if he tries hard enough. The unspoken assumption that permeates their every strategy is that any individual with the right attitude can contribute significantly to social transformation. In fact their publicity is filled with apocryphal accounts that appear to bear this out. It is as if an American born into a Dinka village in South Sudan would somehow find within himself the wherewithal to pull himself up by his boot-straps, put himself through college and become a rocket scientist, and probably train a few others to follow in his footsteps. The reality is, of course, that he would remain a Dinka tribesman herding his cattle the same as everyone else.

The transfer of technology from one culture to another, which is the basis of all social and economic development, is an extremely delicate process, just as transferring an organ from one human being to another is also an extremely delicate process and cannot be guaranteed to work. There are a great many factors involved but the most important one and the one that ironically has been given the least attention is the stance that the host community enjoys vis-a-vis its environment, in particular whether this stance happens to be assertive or compliant in character. An 'assertive' stance is one that has arrogated to itself the right to impose its will on circumstance, as our modern technology-based First World has done; and a 'compliant' stance is one that sees the environment as the dominant partner, as is the case with most poor countries. Social and economic development in its purest form is about the imposition of will on circumstance and this is realised through a cause and effect analysis of circumstance and the application of prescriptions that are scientific and technical in character. Development is mankind's way of saying 'I am not happy with the way things are and I am going to shape them according to my will'.

An extreme but poignant example of wrong-doing would be to try to introduce a mining project into a Bhutanese Buddhist community that has an absolute reverence for nature. We see from this example that technological appropriateness is more than just a matter of matching skills with resources in a sustainable fashion, which in itself is difficult; it is also, and more importantly, about respecting and accommodating the relationship that exists between the host community and its environment. The values that are intrinsic to a given technology, which are cultural in essence, must be compatible with the values of the host community. If they are not technological transfer is not possible. It has been the failure of development agencies to understand the nature and the importance of this relationship that has been at the root of their ineffectiveness.

Development professionals would have done well to have analysed and understood the changes that led to Europe's development and then applied these lessons to the developing world. The first thing they would have noted is that Europe's spectacular advances in science and technology over the past two hundred years were preceded by a shift in popular values from superstition to rational determinism, the impact of which was seismic. Africa is still in the grips of superstition and this, along with tribalism and corruption, constitute what I believe are the major obstacles to Africa's development, all three being deeply rooted in its culture. To provide but one simple example of the scale of the problem that superstition presents - if a man believes that his son died of a neighbour's curse when in fact he died of malaria he is never going to find a cure. The question to be asked is 'what allowed Europe to make this transition from superstition to rational determinism on such a massive scale?' And the answer is 'religion', which in Europe's case was a revived and enlightened Christianity. As the theologian C.S. Lewis remarked 'Mankind became aware that the world was governed by laws when he became aware of the existence of a Law-maker'.

To assume that Europe's development was a natural phenomenon in which the consciousness of the masses played little or no part, as most development experts do, and then suppose that the underdeveloped world would naturally follow suit if they adopted the same technology, which is the basis of most development thinking today, has proven to be a naive and costly mistake. We might note that China's spectacular rise to world power status was preceded by a violent cultural revolution as symbolised by the cutting off of the pigtail. Such a break with the past was necessary if modern ideas were to take root. Chairman Mao's methods were brutal but effective and he clearly understood the relationship between culture and technology. There was, however, a milder and gentler option available to him had he but looked for it, as we shall see in a moment.

All successful technological transfer, therefore, presupposes a compatibility of values or what we might call a 'symbiosis' between the host community and the technology to be introduced. Technological innovation in one form or another is necessary because it is only through technology that the surplus in productivity that is needed for the generation of wealth can take place. For example, in pre industrial society it is estimated that it took twelve families working full-time *on* the land to support one family living *off* the land. After mechanisation arrived this ratio was soon reversed and what is called 'specialisation' appeared, meaning there arose a whole range of skills and trades that brought enrichment and ease to peoples' lives. Symbiosis of this kind occurs spontaneously when a culture is in charge of its own development, as happened in Europe in its industrial revolution, but it is extremely difficult to achieve when a technology is being imposed from the outside, especially when it is imposed by someone who does not fully understand the values of the recipient culture. The subtleties involved would challenge the knowledge of even the most astute anthropologist and most aid workers have neither the time nor the sensitivity to work it out.

There do exist small pockets of the kind of sensitivity that is needed for successful social and economic development but these are far from mainstream; in fact they are generally looked upon by those who do work in mainstream development as belonging to a lunatic fringe. Among the very best is the Dutch 'endogenous' concept which literally means 'development from within' and seeks to design new technologies around cultural values that are already in place.

There is no evidence that a typical Western approach to social and economic development has ever worked. No country has ever built a robust economy on a foundation of aid, the classic example being China which has received precious little development assistance and is now a world power, and Africa which has received countless billions of dollars' worth of development assistance and is still for the most part locked in poverty. The aid industry - and it *is* an industry that includes governments, universities, NGO's, private consultants and so forth - is in large part bogus and a good many people know it. It remains unchallenged, however, because it is no-one's interest to challenge it. Why would anyone risk upsetting the apple cart when so many people are making such a good living out of it? Just to be perfectly clear what we are talking about here let me make a sharp distinction between *emergency or relief assistance* that follows in the wake of a disaster, which is perfectly necessary, valid and laudable; and *social and economic development* which usually is not. Both of these come under the heading of 'Aid'.

The myth of the leader runs deep in our psyche reinforced as it is by countless movies with John Wayne and Clint Eastwood conquering evil single-handedly. It is said of newspaper editors that they end up believing their own headlines; by the same token Americans have ended up believing their own movies. The myth needs to be expunged if we are to correctly understand the process that has brought us to our current global impasse and come up with a solution.

I have used the failure of the multi-million dollar Aid industry to illustrate my point, but the same argument can be applied to our governments. We have invested our leaders in the guise of politicians and economists with the authority to devise and implement policies that have turned out to be at best unsustainable and at worst toxic, while only ever aiming to benefit limited sections of the world's population, and we are now counting the cost. Our imperfect grasp of the dynamics of change has landed us in serious trouble. The key lesson to be drawn from all of this is that if we are to find a way out of our current mess then we should not be looking to individuals to lead the way. Most of the disillusionment that we feel towards our political leaders stems from the fact that we have bought into the myth that gifted individuals have the power to transform our circumstance. They do not.

Let us now, by way of contrast, move on to consider the impact that Islam had on both the people of Arabia and the world at large. As we do this I am conscious that the transition from one perspective to the other may seem abrupt to the point of deserving to be set down as a separate chapter. I have chosen not to do so, however, because I sense that the juxtaposition of the two opposing and contradictory approaches may be helpful. The impact that Islam had on the world speaks directly to our present condition and merits consideration at this point. It is a vast subject and we shall only touch upon it here in the utmost brevity. For those who are interested in an in-depth account of this miraculous event I would recommend the book *Muhammed and the Course of Islam* by Hasan Balyuzi.

Before we do so, however, I would like to mention as an aside that many years ago in the late 1960s I saw a film in a public cinema in London on the life of Prophet Mohammed called The Message. I thought it was an excellent film which portrayed Islam in a very sympathetic light. No-one actually played the part of Prophet Mohammed although the camera took his place on occasions and his followers addressed the camera as if it were the Prophet. I thought it was an innovative and successful way of conveying the station of the Prophet without risking offence to anyone by bringing in a mere human being to play an impossible part. We have seen in the many attempts by actors over the years to capture the essence of Christ just how impossible it is. All of these attempts have failed and what we have been left with is a man, usually a white European with long hair and beard, gazing agonizingly into the middle distance. The film mysteriously disappeared from circulation shortly afterwards and I suspect that it may have been the result of pressure brought to bear on the film distributors by Muslim clerics. If this was the case I believe it was a mistake because the film showed Islam in a favourable light which would be of significant benefit to the Muslim cause if it were around today.

Arabia in the seventh century AD was a chaotic place. Although religious belief descended from the teachings of Abraham who preached monotheism in practice idolatry was rife. Intertribal warfare was also rife with the result that the people lived in constant fear for their lives and the male population was seriously depleted leaving many women with no possibility of finding a husband. The balance was somewhat restored by the fact that a man, if he was rich enough, might have a hundred wives or more but this did little for the status of women. In fact a part of Arabian ritual was the burial of daughters alive for the shame that their existence brought to the father. Arabia at that time was indeed a sad and benighted place.

We might take immediate note that the Islamic provision for a man to have up to four wives represented both a protection and a liberation for women at that time. It was a *protection* because it acknowledged the shortage of men and that a woman might wish to have a husband and a family. And it was a *liberation* because it prevented a woman from becoming one of a hundred wives. It should be noted also that monogamy was not part of original Christian doctrine and it is known, for example, that some of the disciples had more than one wife. Furthermore, Islamic doctrine contains the caveat 'provided he (the husband) treats them equally'. Some modern Islamic scholars have argued that since no-one but Allah could treat people equally what the Prophet was actually advocating was monogamy and that when people were mature enough to understand this would be the time to adopt it. This represents just one of a number of attempts on the part of Islamic scholars to square the teachings of seventh century Arabia with the norms of our modern world.

In the midst of the chaos of Arabia at this time there lived an unschooled merchant who was renowned for his piety and who was later to become known to the world as the Prophet Mohammed. At the age of twenty-five and, unusually, still unmarried because he lacked sufficient wealth to pay a dowry, he married an older woman, perhaps forty years old, named Khadijah who also happened to be his employer. Prophet Mohammed later had two sons, both of whom died, and four daughters who lived.

In 610 AD when Prophet Mohammed was about forty years old the Angel Gabriel appeared to him and announced that he had been chosen as God's Messenger, whereupon he fled for refuge to Khadijah in a state of panic and she wrapped him in a blanket. Thus began the Prophet's mission the first objective of which was to pacify the savage and warring tribes of Arabia and bring them back to the worship of a single God, the same God of the Old and the New Testaments. There is no contradiction in Islam between any of the teachings of the prophets of what Muslims refer to as the Adamic cycle, Adam being considered the first of the prophets of God. Muslims accept the divine missions of all the Old Testament prophets as well as that of Jesus Christ. Mohammed instructed his followers to respect those whom he referred to as 'the people of the Book' meaning those who follow the Bible. In theory, therefore, there are no grounds for Muslims to show hostility towards either Jews or Christians.

Mohammed managed to gather a small band of followers around him and embarked upon the monumental task of disseminating the new religion amidst a people who were truly barbaric. His revelations which were written down at the time on scraps of parchment, leaves, bone, leather and stones were later gathered up, transcribed and compiled into what we know as the Koran which means 'The Recitation'. It was first put together by the Prophet's own relatives in 652 AD about twenty years after His death. Islamic Scripture consists of the Koran which is considered the infallible word of God, and the Hadith or Traditions which were compiled between two and three hundred years after the Prophet's death. The Hadith which are contained in six volumes do not have the same authority as the Koran.

After a great number of setbacks and untold suffering his message eventually took root and his mission to bring unity and monotheism to the peoples of Arabia succeeded. His teachings laid the foundation for a new and vibrant civilisation that within two hundred years had spread throughout the Middle East to the Indus Valley and across Central Asia in the east, and to the Iberian Peninsula, southern Italy and across North Africa in the west. In a recent BBC documentary on the life of the Prophet it was stated that Prophet Mohammed was 'one of the three most influential people to have ever lived'.

The transformative power that was released into the world by the Prophet's divine mission was nothing short of miraculous. No explanation other than what we commonly refer to as a 'miracle', meaning something that has no logical explanation, can come remotely close to accounting for the scale of transformation that took place. In contrast, even the greatest of philosophers have only ever been able to educate and improve the lives of a limited number of people around them. They have never been able to inspire the transition of a whole nation from a state of savagery to advanced civilisation.

We might note two aspects of particular importance. The first is the unfathomable ability of the new religion to create bonds of friendship between formerly entrenched enemies. In this regard we might compare contemporary efforts to establish peaceful relations between Israelis and Palestinians which have employed any number of political strategies and inducements to no tangible effect. The second is the scientific and artistic brilliance of the civilisation that arose on the foundation of Islamic belief. And here we might reflect upon the fact that such brilliance occurred without the intervention of hordes of aid experts brought in from far afield at enormous expense.

The historian Thomas Carlyle describes this mysterious power of the messenger of God in these words:

'The plain truth, very plain, we think is, that....One that has a higher Wisdom, a hitherto unknown spiritual Truth in him, is stronger, not than ten men that have it not, nor than ten thousand, but than all men that have it not; and stands among them with a quite ethereal, angelic power, as if with a sword out of Heaven's own armoury, which no buckler,

and no tower of brass will finally withstand'. Signs of the Times.

At a time when Europe was plunged in its Dark Age and travel was so precarious on account of the robbers and the miserable state of the roads that only the most hardy would even attempt it, many of the roads in the Islamic world were paved and lit and its citizens were able to travel freely and in perfect safety. Brilliant achievements were attained in the arts and sciences. The Islamic world boasted the finest libraries in the world while its centres of learning did much to lay the foundation for our modern medicine, science, architecture and jurisprudence. A number of what we consider to be European discoveries were in fact rediscoveries of the work of Islamic scholars dating back hundreds of years, the circulation of the blood (Harvey), planetary motion (Kepler), and gravity (Newton) being just three examples.

The essential point to be noted from this astonishing explosion of creative energy is that its origin can be traced directly back to the teachings of Prophet Mohammed. Furthermore, as stated above, all the world's divine religions, that is, Hinduism, Judaism, Zoroastrianism, Buddhism, Christianity, Islam, as well as others that have been forgotten in the mists of time, and still others that flourished in the Americas, have had this same effect of giving birth to brilliant civilisations which came to represent the apex of human achievement in their day. All have claimed to derive from the same Source, all have set out to transform mankind, and all have proven their worth.

If religion really is the great force for good that I describe the obvious question to now ask is, 'where did it all go wrong?' The matter of their decline is the subject of the following chapters.

Section 3

WHERE ARE WE NOW?

Chapter Nine

SOCIETY IN DECLINE

We have seen in the case of seventh century Arabia how a spiritual seed can be planted and a new civilisation emerge from it. It will pass through a series of different stages that might be described as the heroic, the formative and the classic which is also its golden age, and then it will start to decline. This is the path that all civilisations must follow; each has its springtime, its summer, its autumn and its winter. The Surih of Jonah in the Koran expresses it like this:

Unto every nation there is a preordained term;
therefore when their term is expired, they shall
not have respite for an hour, neither shall they
be anticipated.

We human beings also follow a similar path of ascent and descent in our individual lives and just as an individual life can be peaceful, happy and productive or it can be turbulent, unhappy and unproductive, so a nation can be the same. Although there is an inexorability about life in any form given that it has a start date and an end date it does not have to be one condition or the other for we have been given control of our destiny and can determine the outcome. We are responsible for our state of being. This may be said of our current situation as a nation which is essentially one of decline. It does not have to be chaotic if we do not want it to be; we have the means to prevent it.

The signs are, however, that we are about to enter a period of chaos and my contention is that it will be destructive to the extent that we have abandoned our spiritual principles and by this I mean those principles that lie at the heart of all divine religion which in our case happens to be Christianity. If we reclaim them and honour them in time, and in sufficient number to form a critical mass of resistance, then we need not suffer unduly. But if we fail to respond appropriately, then the result will be catastrophic and we will be responsible.

The well-known poem by the Irish poet W.B.Yeats entitled *The Second Coming* ably describes the process that unfolds when we lose sight of our spiritual obligations - the falcon represents society and the falconer is the messenger of God.

> *Turning and turning in the widening gyre*
> *The falcon cannot hear the falconer;*
> *Things fall apart; the centre cannot hold;*
> *Mere anarchy is loosed upon the world,*
> *The blood-dimmed tide is loosed, and everywhere*
> *The ceremony of innocence is drowned;*
> *The best lack all conviction, while the worst*
> *Are full of passionate intensity.*

Here we see the process of disintegration that necessarily overtakes society once the light of religion has been extinguished. This is a spiritual law that is absolute and there is no exception to it. I have seen societies disintegrate like this in Africa and I know that the same thing can happen in Britain. Over the past fifty years we have plumbed the depths of decadence in this country and the scene is now set, a scene that will no doubt serve as a lesson to future generations. Spiritual laws apply to everyone; there is no escape clause for the British. If we allow Britain to become a spiritual void we will suffer the fate of Rwanda, Liberia and Sierra Leone. There will be anarchy on our streets; there will be violence and bloodshed; people will barricade themselves inside their homes too afraid to go out; later on they will flee. The best who 'lack all conviction' will look on helplessly while the worst who are 'full of passionate intensity' wreak havoc.

In the full knowledge that any society is only ever one generation away from anarchy we will have allowed it to happen. We have let the genie out of the bottle and now we have to find a way of getting him back in and it is not going to be easy. Perhaps we thought that life was just a game, about 'having a good time' and nothing more, and so it may have seemed for a while but in reality life is anything but a game. My mother always warned me that 'the devil makes work for idle hands' which sounded like good sense to me at the time just as it does now. I mean, you don't need a PhD in behavioural psychology to know that this is true. An Inca ruler speaking five hundred years ago said *'if there is unemployment in the kingdom get the men to move a mountain from one place to another'*. If my mother understood this and a Peruvian Inca understood this how come our modern society does not understand it? Who was the genius in our midst who decided that it was acceptable to pay millions of our citizens to sit around doing nothing all day long? And should we be surprised when the end result is negative?

My mother also told me that 'you need a long spoon to sup with the devil' and I have since discovered that no spoon is ever long enough; you only need to look twice in his direction and he will get you. Not that my mother actually believed in the devil, I hasten to add, she just wanted to warn me about playing with fire; the lower self is a dangerous thing to play around with. It was her version of the Cherokee grandfather's tale. The Islamic Tradition (Hadith) warns us about it in these terms: 'the first look is yours; the second look is Mine'.

When we cease to engage in prayer the spiritual sustenance that flows to our higher self is cut off. At first the effect may not be noticeable and life may go on as normal. We may even feel a sense of liberation at not having to observe a spiritual discipline but the sense of freedom is short-lived. Our attention immediately starts to turn inwards. The first thing to suffer will be our relationships with those closest to us. There will arise an impatience and a lack of consideration that was not there before. It may be nothing serious at first but it is a beginning. Then will come a feeling of dissatisfaction with others, with ourselves and with life in general, accompanied by a tendency to complain. A sense of gratitude for what we have will be replaced by a feeling of resentment for what we do not have. The positive is turning to negative.

These changes will be replicated outside the home in society at large and thereafter we might expect the process of decline to go something like this:

1. People cease to trust each other as before;
2. They become suspicious and fearful;
3. They become less courteous and communicative;
4. They become less caring;
5. They begin to conceal their motives;
6. They become more self-centred and greedy;
7. They start to scheme;
8. They become corrupt;
9. Crime increases;
10. Many feel they have to take extra measures to protect themselves with locks, burglar alarms, security lights, even weapons;
11. Schism develops between individuals, families, groups;
12. Interested parties band together for protection;
13. The sense of threat increases;
14. A spark ignites a conflagration;
15. Conflict erupts and society breaks down.
16. Anarchy prevails.

The most difficult thing for me to accept about our decline has always been the part played by sociologists and psychologists many of whom have often encouraged and sanctioned the very conduct that has brought it about. Each new step downwards has been applauded, from the first use of the B-word in Pygmalion, to the first public utterance of the F-word in the 1968 movie M.A.S.H., to our present day where obscenity is all around. How can it be considered progress when the obscene language that is now the norm in films and television is heard in our schools and used by pupils who are out of control? I considered becoming a teacher myself at one time and even completed a Certificate in Education course at Manchester University in 1973. I had second thoughts when a visiting lecturer made the unusually bold statement to a conference hall filled with aspiring young teachers 'there has been a war in our schools between the pupils and the teachers and the pupils have won'. He confirmed what I already knew to be the case that the lower self was fast gaining the ascendancy in our society and that our classrooms had become the front line.

It is said that the average child in the United States by the time he reaches ten years old has seen five thousand murders on the screen. I recall only too well hearing of a child soldier in Sierra Leone, a boy of seven or eight years old who grew up in war, when asked if he had ever killed anyone, replied 'no, they just fall down'. Should we be surprised if a ten year old boy in the United States or Britain develops a similar irreverence for the sanctity of human life? Should it come as a surprise when we hear that there are seventeen thousand homicides a year in the United States?

It is worth taking a look at how the media works to see how this indiscipline has come about. A simple example will suffice. I was watching a movie on John Lennon's adolescent years recently entitled 'Nowhere Boy'. There is a scene in which he steals half a dozen records from a shop and then throws most of them away keeping just the one that he wants. It struck me that if Lennon's behaviour was not immediately condemned outright by someone in authority it would serve as a model for others to copy. Since the film does not allow for any feedback, the act of theft stands alongside every other aspect of the life of someone who has acquired the status of a pop legend as something to be admired and copied. We do not need to analyse why this should be, we just know that it is so. It is the same principle that underpins advertising and advertising, as we all know, works.

Given that it would be impossible to have instant feedback on every single detail that takes place in a film it is clear that the moral tide is running in favour of the film director. Multiply this by a thousand times or a million times and it adds up to a barrage of anti social behaviour that leaves decent, law-abiding citizens feeling helpless and demoralised. The common retort of those who endorse such behaviour 'to switch the television off if you don't like it' does not solve the problem because if such behaviour finds its way into our everyday lives, as it has done, then switching off the television is not an answer.

The media not only subverts it covers its tracks and it does so by attaching false labels to our actions to the point that I find myself wondering if there has ever been such a reluctance to 'call a spade a spade'. We hear that 1968, for example, was a summer of 'love' when in fact it was a summer of sex; we are warned that 'the next programme contains 'strong' language' when in fact what it contains is obscene language; and we are warned about the 'adult' humour that is about to follow when what we really mean is adolescent humour given that no self-respecting adult would stoop so low for laughs. We are now so used to such phrases that they trip effortlessly off the tongue and we no longer question them. In this last regard we might stop and reflect that none of the great comedians of the past resorted to obscenities for laughs; in sharp contrast to today's less talented comics whose every other word is an obscenity from which we may conclude that obscenity is the first resort of the second rate comedian.

In former times up until the late 1950's the major influences in the lives of young people were their parents, their school teachers and the church minister, always assuming that they went to church which statistically speaking was improbable. Of these the most important was the home or as the Chinese philosopher Confucius so neatly put it *'the strength of a nation derives from the integrity of the home'*. Such people were considered the pillars of society and could be relied upon to provide sound guidance. Then mass media came along and entered our homes supplanting the influence of the parents, with the avant-garde of the art world in close attendance and the world of behavioural psychology not far behind, most of whom seemed committed to the notion that whatever could dredged up from our subconscious had to be valid by virtue of the fact that it was there. The slate was now cleared for anyone to write on it whatever he wanted and no one was in a position to stop it.

Very soon our private thoughts that were at one time controllable passed into the public domain where they gained acceptance and thereafter became uncontrollable, and then multiplied until they formed the critical mass that constitutes the social norms of today. Such is the route that deviancy takes to establish itself in our midst. I often think that there is something to be said for 'taboo' because once something has been voiced it becomes an option in our repertoire of possibilities and when this happens the media will seize upon it and use it to its advantage. What is it that Buddhists say, 'see no evil, hear no evil, speak no evil'? I believe there is wisdom in these words.

The major influences in our lives, therefore, passed from those who had a strong commitment to the well-being of society to those who had none at all so that today we can say in all fairness that society's destiny is in the hands of people who do not care. It is no good looking to the media industry to regulate itself because it will never do it; the profit motive is too strong. Apart from news broadcasts and documentaries that seek to inform, the primary goal of the media is to distort, whether for entertainment purposes or to sell products and this they do more often than not by appealing to our lower nature. A classic example is to be found in the way that perfumes and deodorants are advertised which would be comic were it not so debauched. Next time you see one please ask yourself 'what do those images on the screen have to do with an odour?'

The forgoing begs the question as to what constitutes a good society and this is a question that I prefer to answer in a negative way, that is, by saying what a good society is not. For example, a society that does not have murder must be considered higher than a society that does have murder; a society that does not have corruption must be considered higher than a society that does have corruption; a society that does not have rape must be considered higher than a society that does have rape; a society that does not have paedophilia must be considered higher than a society that does have paedophilia; a society that does not have drug addiction must be considered higher than a society that does have drug-addiction; a society that does not have alcoholism must be considered higher than a society that does have alcoholism; a society that does not have prostitution must be considered higher than a society that does have prostitution; and so on with other traits such as lying, obscenity, violence, theft, vandalism, domestic violence - in fact the list seems endless. A 'good' society, by definition, will be none of the above.

The absence of such things is a measuring stick against which we can determine whether or not Britain is a healthy society. When we do the evidence suggests that Britain is not a healthy society at all; in fact the contrary is true, that Britain is a very sick society. All the signs are present of a society that has turned its back on its spiritual heritage and is heading for disaster. In Bristol where I grew up fifty years ago such things were not present. Crime was virtually non-existent and we in Bristol, like most people in Britain, did not even bother to lock our doors. All this change has come about in fifty years. If we project this trend forwards by another fifty years what might we expect? I think we know the answer; the answer is Rwanda, Liberia and Sierra Leone. The One who made us is no racist, nor is He any respecter of persons. His laws apply to the totality of humankind and we respect them or we disrespect them at our peril.

If we take a look at another culture in decline so as to compare and contrast it might provide us with a clearer understanding of what is happening with us right now. Britain's situation is complex and depressing but it is by no means without its redeeming features. The classic comparison is that of Rome and it is relevant because Rome like Britain also boasted a vast empire that was all-powerful in its day and then underwent a process of gradual but irreversible decline.

The decline of Rome was compounded by the accession to the throne of a deranged emperor named Commodus who alienated those close to him and pushed his subjects too far until they finally rebelled en masse. The closing line of the movie The Decline and Fall of the Roman Empire is 'a great civilisation is not conquered from without until it has destroyed itself from within'. This statement is true to a certain extent but it is not the whole story. All civilisations, as we noted above, are subject to decline regardless of who is in charge because nothing lasts forever, not even mighty empires. Britain's days as an empire were also numbered and its time was destined to run out sooner or later. Thankfully we have never had a deranged dictator at the helm to accelerate the process but there were other factors. The First and Second World Wars were probably our equivalent in that they bankrupted the nation and brought the curtain down on Empire prematurely.

Britain's empire was different in many respects from that of Rome. Whenever possible Britain employed a system of indirect rule which left the customs, the language and the power structures of the countries it colonised in place so that its rule may be said to have been generally benign in comparison. It was certainly never the crushing omnipresence of Rome. This may come as something of a shock to those who have been brought up on a diet of Marxism which has always equated colonialism with oppression but this was seldom the case, at least not where Britain was concerned. I have spent over twenty years working in Africa in countries that have included the former colonies of Tanzania, Kenya, Uganda, Sierra Leone, Nigeria, and also Sudan which was not strictly speaking a colony although its status was similar, and I have only very rarely come across any ill feeling towards the British. I have heard plenty of ill feeling towards their own governments but precious little towards the British. On the contrary, I have heard considerable appreciation for the British legacy of Christianity, formal education, modern medicine and honest government, and also for a language that allows those who speak it to engage freely with the world community. I have also worked in former French, Portuguese, Spanish and German colonies and found that the citizens were not nearly so forthcoming in their praise for their colonial masters. I recall one comment in particular that a Sudanese friend made when I asked him why the Sudanese are still fond of the British and he replied without hesitation, 'because when we asked you to leave, you left'. It said a lot about Britain's style of governance.

I do not believe that the British presence in Africa was ever an impediment to Africa's development. As mentioned in Chapter Eight, my own conclusion concerning Africa's failure to develop economically and socially is that three major obstacles stand in its way and these are: superstition, tribalism and corruption, all of which are rife in sub Saharan Africa. The argument in its simplest form goes like this: superstition – if you believe that your son died of a neighbour's curse when in fact he died of malaria you are never going to find a cure; tribalism – tribalism is by definition an obstacle to the social cohesion that is a prerequisite for any successful social and economic development; and corruption - if the money that is supposed to go to schools and hospitals ends up in the private bank account of government ministers what chance is there of a country progressing? The British presence represented an antidote to all three of these conditions and far from the colonial presence being the obstacle to development that many of Britain's critics would have us believe, it was actually an enormous advantage. It set Africa on the right path as many Africans today are quick to acknowledge.

Neither has Britain had to suffer the scourge of dictatorship, deranged or otherwise, like other colonial powers such as Germany, Italy, France, Spain, Portugal and the Soviet Union. Our democratic institutions protected us from this. I sometimes think that what is keeping Britain going now, and is protecting us from an even worse fate, are all the atrocities that we could have committed when we were in a position to do so but seldom did.

A Roman senator said 'an empire starts to die when its people no longer believe in it' and this has certainly been true of Britain. In the 1950's a good many Britons sensed the waning of the spirit that had held the Empire together and decided to pack their bags and head for Canada, Australia and New Zealand uttering sentiments like 'this is no longer the country I grew up in'. Others stayed but with an increasingly negative mindset towards their country.

Interestingly, the latest film by the American director, Michael Moore, 'Capitalism: A love Affair', which may well turn out to be a major landmark in American cinema history, compares the decline of the United States with that of the Roman Empire. I believe that the comparison of Rome and the United States is more relevant than that of Rome and Britain even though America's influence has always been more economic than political. The unchecked capitalism of American society has seen the emergence of a dangerous wealth gap with the unrepentant super-rich on one side, whose personal fortunes run into billions, and the impoverished and dispossessed masses on the other who can barely make ends meet. What we see is a dog-eat-dog social order that is driven by the laws of socio-economic Darwinism in which the bosses are all-powerful and the employees have few rights. The film argues that the poor in the United States are being pushed by their tightening circumstances to the point of revolt.

The destiny of the British Empire was one thing and the destiny of the British people is another. Britain's enemy today is itself and its pain is self-inflicted. We have no one to blame for our predicament but ourselves, although it is undeniable that we have had more than a little help from our friends across the Atlantic in the form of a barrage of pornography and violence that came originally from Hollywood but which we have since learned to manufacture ourselves. There can be little doubt that Hollywood has been a major destabilising influence in our fortunes although at the end of the day we will have to admit that it was we who allowed it to happen and so it is we who are therefore responsible. Our failure to re-act constructively has its roots somewhere between cowardice and ignorance. I find it strange that so few people seem to see a relationship between this media onslaught and our social decline. Perhaps I see it more clearly because I have seen first-hand how innocent communities in other parts of the world have been quickly and easily destabilised by it in circumstances that make the impact all the more stark.

What is especially pernicious about this media onslaught is that there is no way of stopping it. I have often thought that Al Qaeda might well gain a modicum of sympathy if it were to justify its attacks in terms of a war against the moral pollution that pours continuously from the giant sewer called 'Hollywood'. I suspect that this may be in their minds when they refer to the United States as 'Great Satan'; they just need to articulate it a bit better. I have yet to see one shred of awareness amongst American politicians that this might possibly be the reason for the United States being attacked. All we have ever heard from them is that the members of Al Qaeda are 'terrorists' and 'enemies of freedom'. Their minds seem to switch off at this point. How I long for someone to stand up and shout out, Ronald-Reagan style, 'Mr. Obama shut down this sewer!' And to hear the reply 'sorry folks, we can't do it, not in a free society', which will speak volumes about our notions of freedom and where it is taking us.

How do we prevent our society from descending into anarchy? Well, this is what this book is all about, identifying the disease and prescribing the remedy, but we are not ready for the definitive answer just yet. We will come to it in good time after we have considered a few other aspects of our present predicament. The interim answer is that the only antidote is to be found in divine religion and that we all, as individuals, must re-engage with the spiritual and moral principles that it contains. But this is no easy task. The path has been obscured for us by meddling intellectuals who may mean well - although I am not entirely sure about this - but are proving to be more of a hindrance than a help.

Just one example of this may serve to illustrate the point. Not long ago I was watching a programme on TV in UK called Time Watch. It began with the presenter stating as a categorical fact that 'we are here on this earth by chance'. Such statements as this have become so commonplace nowadays that few seem to question them; they have become part of the received wisdom of our culture. A more balanced view would surely go something like this:

'There are many people in the world who adhere to a divine religion and such people who make up the vast majority of the people on our planet, about ninety percent in fact, believe that we have been created by a divine being whom we call 'God' and that there is a purpose to our existence. There is also a small minority of people like myself, however, who believe that there is no God and that there is no purpose to our existence and that we are here by chance. We are, as I say, a small minority and there is every chance that we could be wrong but this is how we see it'.

Now, this would be a more fair and balanced approach, would it not? What does the presenter think the impact on our children and our youth is likely to be when he tells them categorically that 'we are here by chance?' For a start it is going to create a sense of insecurity which he has no right to do under any circumstances; and secondly, it is likely to promote a mindset that says 'well, if this is all there is I might as well make the most of it' and we can imagine what sort of consequences this might bring. In fact it brings us right to the third harmful myth of our time, the myth that we are on this earth to satisfy whatever desires we happen to have, when in fact nothing could be further from the truth. Our life's purpose is to acquire those qualities that will ensure our happiness in the life that follows this one and this implies, above all else, learning to become detached from what is around us.

And then there is the scientific value of the statement itself. I recall in this connection a comment made by a fifteen year old schoolgirl in relation to the Big Bang theory. She said 'every explosion I have ever heard of has caused chaos; how come this one caused perfect order?' Not a bad question for a fifteen year old and I for one would like to hear the presenter's answer.

Chapter Ten

RELIGION IN DECLINE

We have seen how society breaks down when the spiritual power that has been holding it together wanes. Now we will take a look at religion and consider what happens once it has passed its golden age. We shall need to back-track a little.

We noted in Chapter Six that Christianity has lost much of its original vigour and that no amount of exhortation from its leaders can bring it back. Attempts at a revival are being made with assistance mainly from American evangelists and also from what is being termed 'reverse missionaries', a remarkable phenomenon whereby missionaries from Africa are now coming to Britain to teach us the Christianity that we no longer practice; they are 'returning the favour', as it were. But the effect is limited. This is not necessarily a reflection of the capacity of the preachers themselves, nor is it necessarily a reflection of the decline in spiritual practice of the British people which we know to be a fact. It is rather because of religion's social dimension which, as previously explained, is designed to atrophy after a certain number of years so that it can be replaced by another with greater vigour that will inspire an ever-evolving humanity to new heights of achievement. Atrophy is built into the Divine plan.

Let me recap briefly so that we know exactly where we stand. There are two aspects to any religion: there is the one that may be said to constitute its *spiritual* core which teaches love, compassion, generosity, forgiveness, honesty, responsibility, truthfulness, trustworthiness and so on. This aspect which is found in all the world's religions is eternal and unchanging. The other aspect is its *social* dimension which recognises that humankind is constantly evolving and is in need of new laws that correspond to its current state of development. Each messenger of God has brought laws that are designed uniquely for his particular dispensation and these are only intended to last until the next messenger of God comes along and replaces them with new ones that are appropriate for the new age.

Any attempt to sustain and apply the laws of a former dispensation to a later one has a tendency to end in extremism because it is ultimately impossible to achieve, as we are witnessing right now in the attempts by certain Muslim sects to impose 'Sharia' law on a modern world that bears scant resemblance to seventh century Arabia. Similarly, certain Islamic teachings on economics are incompatible with the kind of large scale investment that modern business often calls for. For example, while it is permitted for Muslims to engage in private transactions it is not permitted to pool labour and resources to form corporations. It is true that certain countries like Indonesia and Malaysia which are seen to represent a 'softer version' of Islam have somehow managed to reconcile these differences but Middle Eastern countries have not.

In sum, the dispensation of Christ confirmed and built upon the teachings of Moses, and the dispensation of Prophet Mohammed confirmed and built upon the teachings of Christ. Similarly the teachings of the Buddha confirmed and built upon the teachings of Krishna. Each new messenger of God confirms the basic message of his predecessor while introducing new laws for his day and in so doing he brings new potential to our knowledge, our creativity and our social organisation. It is not intended that our condition should remain static. Knowledge and perfection are endless and it is our destiny to pursue them both. There is nothing defective in this design. On the contrary, it represents a perfect symmetry of purpose.

The foundation of all civilisation, however, remains forever rooted in those primary values that lie at the heart of each of the world's religions. The same stabilising power that is found in any one of them is to be found in all of them. Those who claim that only their own religion provides the true answer to life do so because they have never seriously looked at any of the others. Exclusivity is not part of the divine plan. If this essential similarity between the religions were properly understood it would not be necessary for governments to consider removing religious instruction from our school curriculum for fear of causing division between pupils from different ethnic backgrounds. All religion is one, just as the human race is one, and our education system will hopefully one day recognise this.

At present the world is witnessing a dual process of decline, one that is both social and spiritual in nature, namely, the decline of what is commonly referred to as 'Western Civilisation' as well as a decline in religious belief generally. The Bible talks of this time and refers to it as the 'end of the age'. It was formerly translated from the Greek as the 'end of the world', but this was a mistranslation. The Greek word used was 'aeon', which means 'age'. Had the intention been to speak of the end of the 'world' the Greek word would have been 'cosmos'. What I believe we are witnessing in our present turmoil is the end of one age and the birth of another, or the death-throes of one type of civilisation and the birth pangs of another, and on a scale and at a speed that humankind has never experienced before.

What is particularly remarkable about this monumental upheaval is that most of us are remaining in full possession of our faculties while it is happening, as if such a transition were a perfectly normal event. Just imagine - that it supposedly took mankind half a million years to learn how to domesticate fire and yet here we are right now doubling our knowledge every six months and we accept it as perfectly normal!

And there is another monumental change that is taking place right now, one that is equally remarkable and which has also gone virtually unnoticed, which is that at the present time there are no wars going on between sovereign states. When we look back to the last century, which was not very long ago, and we reflect upon the fact that wars between nations were the norm and accounted for the deaths of something like one hundred and fifty million of our fellow human beings, this represents a change of revolutionary proportions. Such a radical transformation in our habits in such a short space of time should be taken as an indication that something earth-shaping is going on and that it is probably not we who are responsible for it. We might wish to claim the credit for it but past evidence, which stretches back to the dawn of time, would indicate that we ourselves are not capable of effecting such a transformation in our nature, let alone in the space of a couple of decades. I venture to suggest that something unprecedented in human experience is going on, something far greater than we human beings can even begin to imagine. We will explore what this might be in a later chapter.

What might we expect from our current crop of religious leaders in the years ahead? If they have humility, as most clergymen and women in Britain thankfully do, then we might expect them to acknowledge their inability to explain contemporary events within the terms of reference that their Faith provides and to continue to pray for the well being of their fellow men and women. This would be the honourable response.

If they do not have humility then we might expect them to engage in the kind of impassioned rhetoric that predicts the salvation of those who think like they do and the come-uppance of those who do not, and even, as a worst case scenario, conspiring to bring it about. This would be the dishonourable response. There is a fine line between using one's God-given talents to promote God's message and using God's message to promote one's God-given talents. Some have crossed this line unknowingly and continue about their business while others have already paid dearly for it in the form of public scandal. Humility is at the heart of true belief. As the thirteenth-century Islamic mystic Jalal al-Din Rumi wrote:

Try to be a sheet of paper with nothing on it;
Be a spot of ground where nothing is growing;
Where something might be planted,
A seed possibly, from the Absolute.

The institutions of religion will necessarily become enfeebled and their influence will continue to diminish. As the divine spirit wanes so gaps will begin to appear in people's beliefs causing them to question things that seemed to make perfect sense before. These gaps were always there but it was possible to ignore them as long as the spirit was strong, just as a man in love will see no flaws in the woman he loves - gaps such as Original Sin, the Trinity and the Physical Resurrection which were never part of Christ's teachings but later became incorporated as if they were.

Mankind is incapable of grasping the full measure of the cause of God no matter how hard he tries; he needs a messenger of God to explain it to him. The Buddha has given us the analogy of the blind men feeling the body of the elephant to illustrate this point. One feels the trunk, another feels a tusk, another feels a leg, another feels the tail and each one believes that he has grasped the truth of what an elephant is but none is successful.

The prophet Daniel is told in no uncertain terms to abandon his attempt to unravel the mysteries of the Holy Scriptures for these will not be revealed until 'the time of the end':

But you, O Daniel, shut up the words, and seal the book, even to the time of the end: many shall run to and fro, and knowledge shall be increased. (Daniel chapter 12 verse 4).

A brief description of what 'the time of the end' is going to be like is provided so that we might recognise it when we see it: *'many shall run to and fro, and knowledge shall be greatly increased.'* And when we add to it a second prophecy: *'the chariots shall rage in the streets, they shall jostle one against another in the broad ways: they shall seem like torches, they shall run like the lightnings!'* (Nahum 2:3,4), then one does not need to be Sherlock Holmes to work out that if the time of the end is not already with us, then it cannot be far away.

The followers of religion will endeavour to fill the gaps in their understanding in different ways. Some will seek out new messages of hope wherever it might be found, perhaps in other faiths or among the plethora of new sects and cults that arise in response to a pressing need for answers. Others who are disillusioned with religion in general may re-engage with the secular world while still keeping one foot in the church, mosque or temple as if to cover their options. It can be a trying time.

Some will continue to profess an undying commitment to their particular faith but, as we have just seen, this can only be done at the expense of reason for none of the traditional faiths has anything relevant to say to our modern world with its myriad complexity. It is the time of the extremist, the last throw of the dice before 'Armageddon', 'Judgement Day' and the 'Day of Reckoning' as they bet their all on an apocalyptical event that will prove them right and all the others wrong. They are God's chosen people, or so the zealots among them believe, which is alarming because zealotry is a flame that no power on earth appears able to extinguish. The number of suicide bombers coming forward to offer their services is not diminishing but increasing.

Zealots are unmoved by any form of reason, threat or inducement. Their sole mission is to find favour in the sight of God. They are beyond the reach of anything that the world can bring to bear. It is a dangerous time.

It is precisely because religion is so vital to us that it generates such intense passion. Most of us recognise that we need religion, certainly on a personal level, and others of us recognise that we need it on a social level also. The fear of the void is abhorrent to most of us. There may be individuals who are happy to exist within a spiritual vacuum, or so they claim, but my personal view is that such affirmations of independence usually derive from a false sense of security. My years of working in conflict zones in Africa have told me that just about everyone who is in dire need turns to a Higher Being for help. I suspect that those who profess to feeling no pull in this direction have yet to be tested. But it is OK, they will learn to appreciate their fallibility when the time comes, and they may even undergo a change of heart and turn out to be the champions of the spirit that the world so badly needs. We shall never know until it happens and even then it will be a private matter between the individual and his Creator.

Others will backslide and turn increasingly to material substitutes for their sustenance but they are on a losing streak on two accounts: firstly because the one can never replace the other; and secondly because their will-power will be no match for the hungry lower self and the appetites they arouse. They may eventually lose contact with their faith altogether and cease to be a force for good and become instead a force for bad. The equilibrium of society is directly dependent for its survival upon the existence of a critical mass of positive values to counter what is negative around us. This critical mass can only ever be composed of people of good faith and the withdrawal of even a single man or woman of substance is a cause for concern.

I saw this clearly when I was in Rwanda and I reflected upon the genocide of 1994 which saw 900,000 Tutsis and moderate Hutus murdered in the space of three months and I asked myself how many more moderate Hutus it would have taken to prevent the massacre from taking place? The ethnic split in this tiny country of six million at the time was ninety percent Hutu and ten percent Tutsis. There must have been a minimum number of moderate Hutus whose good faith would have been sufficient to prevent the tragedy from happening. How many was it, one million, two million, three million, four million? It is of such a critical mass that I speak. Every society everywhere is dependent upon such a critical mass for its survival. When the critical mass of good represents a majority of the citizenry, then there is stability. But when the critical mass of good represents a minority then society is under threat and risks fragmentation. The commitment of every single soul to a higher purpose, therefore, has a direct effect on the stability of the society to which he belongs. The question of whether a person believes in a God or not is not an issue that affects him alone; it affects us all for our destiny is intertwined.

This is what makes our day so special. Humankind cannot live without religion and neither can it live with the wrong interpretation of religion. This means that the onus on us to get it right is critical and this presupposes that there lies within a majority of us a faculty to recognise what is right when we see it. Our survival depends on such a critical mass of right belief being reached.

Each of the messengers of God has promised that at a pre-ordained time, the exact day and hour of which is unknown, there will appear a great spiritual teacher who will usher in a golden age of peace and stability for the whole world. He has been variously referred to as: the return of Krishna (Hinduism); the Lord of Hosts (Judaism); the Lord of the Age (Zoroastrianism); the Fifth Buddha (Buddhism);

the Spirit of Truth and the Return of Christ (Christianity); and the Mahdi, the Q'aim or the Twelfth Imam (Islam). The exact manner of his return and what he will do when he gets here is the subject of debate within each of the respective religions. What is clear, however, is that the level of expectation surrounding the arrival of this great spiritual teacher, which has been with us for well over a hundred years now, is growing by the day.

Chapter 11

CURRENCY AND CULTURE

Money is all about trust. It is, after all, just a piece of paper which has no value in itself which means that people have to believe in it for it to work. The question is - what is it exactly that they believe in? This is a profound question but the answer may not be too difficult to find. Just think of the people that you know and then ask yourself whether or not you trust them and why. We believe in people when the quality of their words matches the quality of their deeds. Our bank notes are like our words and we believe in them when they are backed by honesty and integrity and the more there is of both the more they are worth. Trust is a single commodity and it applies to both people and currency.

Ten years ago I wrote a book entitled *The Day of the Dragon* which recounted my experiences working in war-torn West Africa and I noted in passing that the euro was not a credible currency. Although I had no background in economics, somehow amid the debris of the countries that were collapsing around me, Sierra Leone, Liberia and Guinea, I caught sight of a relationship between the solidity of culture and the solidity of currency and I concluded that the euro would not last because it lacked the credentials that a currency needs for people to believe in it. It seemed to me that culture and currency were inextricably linked in ways that could not be defined by economic terms alone. The present furore surrounding the survival of the euro in which it is hard to find two people who agree on what needs to be done has only served to confirm this view.

There appears to be a general consensus that if the euro is to be saved there has to be what economists call a 'full fiscal union' among the seventeen states that make up the euro zone. What they do not seem able to agree upon is how this full fiscal union should be reached. There is recognition that political union must be a part of it, and this is correct, but a political union alone will not suffice. There was political union in the Soviet Union for over half a century backed by enormous natural resources and a massive population, yet its currency was never credible as the existence of a dual exchange rate and a thriving black market indicated. The type of union that is needed to validate a currency is far deeper and more complex than can be provided by political forces alone. To be fair there is recognition of this point also with some economists arguing that no amount of political or fiscal intervention will work unless confidence is established first. They are correct in their assertion and to understand how such confidence might be established we shall need to enter realms other than politics and economics.

For a currency to be credible the people who use it must believe in it implicitly and for this to happen it must be backed by a culture that is genuinely cohesive, one that is homogeneous in nature. This implies that there has to be a shared value system, which implies in turn that there has to be a shared belief system and that this shared belief system has been adopted by the people of their own free will. In other words, the supporting culture has to be monolithic in character with everyone wilfully sharing a common set of values. You cannot, for example, have disparate communities with significantly differing values sharing ownership of the same currency, just as you cannot have two teams playing the same game according to two different sets of rules. This is the problem that Greece is posing within the euro zone right now; it is playing by a different set of rules. For the record, Greek debt as of the time that this book goes to press, involves figures that are outside the realm of anything that any economy has ever had to deal with in history, and this, by general consent, is the result of Greece's fiscal indiscipline.

The political response to this indiscipline has been to call for Greece to be brought into line but for this to happen there would have to be an overriding authority which those using the currency recognise and respect. At the present time no such authority exists and herein lies the problem because there needs to be one. In theory you could have a government without a currency but you could never have a currency without a government. It was originally thought that the European Commission would perform this policing role through the Stability and Growth Pact which would impose limits on national spending but for this to happen the governments of the member states would have to surrender their sovereignty at least in part to Brussels, and even if the governments were willing to do this it is doubtful that their electorates would accept it.

Most likely the electorates would interpret any attempt at corrective action as an 'interference in their internal affairs' and this is because they would see the directives of the European Commission as coming from an alien body, one that is not truly representative of Greek values. And they would be right because the policies of the European Commission as represented in this instance by the European Central Bank are driven by northern European countries that happen to have Triple 'A' credit ratings. There seems to have been an assumption early on in the life of the euro that the culture underpinning its value would be that of Germany which we know is not the case. What we have now is a house divided and a house divided will sooner or later fall taking its currency down with it.

In brief, the worth of a currency is a direct reflection of the worth of the culture that owns it - the more solid the culture the more solid the currency. For a culture to flourish it must believe in itself implicitly. It needs to know that it is on the right track and that it is going somewhere of significance and for this to happen it needs to be unified in thought and purpose. What is needed for the euro to become a credible currency is a homogenizing agent, something that will bring people together in authentic union and inspire them to greater heights and this is not something that can be achieved by force, coercion, inducement or legislation. The homogenizing agent that has par excellence inspired people and brought them together in authentic union down the ages is religion. This is what the word religion means; it derives from the Latin 'religio' meaning 'to bind together'. In fact religion is the only force known to man that is capable of generating the level of trust needed to make a currency genuinely credible.

The United States dollar bears the words 'In God We Trust' and this is not fortuitous. If the US dollar has been the strongest currency in the world and still is the world's reserve currency it is primarily because the United States as a nation has been built on Christian values - *genuine* Christian values, that is - which the generality of the people have taken to heart and put into everyday practice, as opposed to just paying lip service to them. It could never be possible to do it the other way round - for example, to introduce a new currency with, say, 'Heaven Help Us' written on it, impose it from the outside and expect it to work. This would be naiveté itself. For a currency to be credible it has to emerge as the spontaneous expression of its people and it has to be backed by a uniformity of cultural values that share the same priorities.

Unfortunately the United States has lost its way in recent times and as a consequence the dollar is losing its value. Its strength has waned as the nation has succumbed to non-Christian values. Greed is now considered a national virtue and success is reckoned in the amassing of private fortunes that count in the billions of dollars. At the same time millions struggle to survive on pennies and hand-outs as tens of thousands of decent, hardworking people are needlessly laid off from their jobs with many losing their homes in the process. The United States can no longer be considered a Christian nation. Added to this is corporate corruption that runs right across the business spectrum affecting, inter alia, armaments, oil and above all finance which is where our current crisis began as devious individuals got rich quick out of what is now termed 'leverage', which is a euphemism for moving money from one place to another to no productive end. On top of this there has been increasing involvement of big business in the political process with corporations supporting and influencing politicians on an unprecedented scale. And then there is the Federal Reserve Bank's habit of printing money to finance the national debt which is now too big to be managed legitimately and threatens to cause hyperinflation.

When all of this is added together we begin to understand why the 'almighty dollar' is no longer 'almighty'. In fact today it is barely able to stand on its own. If Saudi Arabia were to withdraw its three trillion dollars from the US stock exchange and its one trillion dollars from US banks, and if China were to convert its US dollars into euros, the US economy would collapse. And collapse, let us not forget, can, like the Twin Towers, be sudden - a catastrophe that might be taken now as a portent of things to come. All of this has come about because the United States has lost its moral compass and with it, its social cohesion. Its recovery is only possible to the extent that the American people reclaim the same values that once made the nation great.

A dissolute culture cannot produce a credible currency; a credible currency can only come from a credible culture. If the attendant culture is not credible then you end up with the Monopoly money that we have seen in Latin America over the years where the money supply bears scant relation to the productive capacity of the nation and governments have been allowed to flout the laws of economics with impunity by printing new money whenever they felt like it, as if money itself – the piece of paper – had some intrinsic value. I happened to be working in Bolivia when the value of the peso slipped from twelve pesos to the dollar to over two million pesos to the dollar and it is an experience that one is unlikely to forget or ever wish to see repeated. In this instance the International Monetary Fund intervened and a new currency, the Boliviano, was introduced at a rate of 2.5 Bolivianos to the dollar along with stringent controls. For the present the medicine appears to be working although it has been a painful recovery which is far from over.

We witnessed the impotence of leaders to control economic forces in the last century with the collapse of communism. Communism failed as an economic system because when something belongs to everyone it belongs to no one and no one cares. Communism was too idealistic and did not take into account human nature as it really is; furthermore it was imposed by force. Capitalism is about to suffer a similar fate but for different reasons. In Capitalism people care too much - for themselves, and if left unchecked powerful individuals will amass fortunes at the expense of the masses for whom they care little. It was always a myth that the wealth would trickle down in sufficient measure to the ones below; it never has.

There is also an element of simple common sense to all of this which does not demand a doctorate in economics to appreciate. If the Chinese economy is booming right now it is because the Chinese themselves are hardworking, disciplined and properly trained which are sound principles by anybody's reckoning. We British are none of these. We used to be but we are not now. The British cannot compete in the electronics industry, for example, not because we lack the investment or the manpower, nor even because the cost of labour is prohibitive, but because we lack the discipline. We also lack the humility. Just imagine what the reaction would be if, in order to sell our products we British were told that we had to speak fluent Mandarin or Japanese and that our children would not be allowed to leave school until they could! This is not to say that the British are any less capable than the Chinese or Japanese – we have proven our worth down the ages - but it is to say that we have become lazy and effete. Our pride has turned to arrogance, our industry has turned to idleness, and our intellectual power has turned its gaze overseas in search of environments where it is valued and respected and can function to its full capacity.

The BBC World Service recently ran a series of debates concerning the future of English as an international language and asked if the relevance of English is diminishing in keeping with the declining US dollar and whether it is likely to be replaced by Mandarin in conformity with the growing strength of the Chinese currency, the yuan. While there is a clear connection between the strength of a currency and the usefulness of the language that goes with it, the argument does not end there. There is also a moral dimension to the debate which the BBC chose not to examine. Britain and the United States, along with other English-speaking nations, occupy a position of pre-eminence on two accounts, the first being the stance that they took in the two World Wars of the last century, and the second being the values that are enshrined in their democratic systems. The two attract strong loyalty.

The worth of a language, therefore, is linked to the moral values of the culture that speaks it just as the worth of a currency is linked to the moral values of the culture that owns it. Evidence of this can be found in the fact that few nations were interested in adopting either the Russian language or the rouble even when the Soviet Union was at its height because they were repelled by the values of a state that was based on propaganda and brutality. What is more likely to undermine the world's interest in maintaining English as an international language is the moral laxity of the English-speaking nations. The BBC World Service might want to reflect upon this as it continues to push its liberal agenda amongst a still largely conservative-minded listening audience. The media, far from being neutral, plays an important role in defining the standards that underpin the strength of both language and currency.

The lesson to be taken from all of this is that economics is essentially a spiritual matter which means that it is our honesty and integrity that determine whether or not an economic system is going to work and that as such it is beyond the capacity of politicians and economists to adequately control. If the professors at the London School of Economics and Harvard Business School had emphasised this moral dimension of economics over and above such matters as the law of supply and demand, marketing strategies and profit margins it is doubtful that the world would be in its current mess. Indeed, they would have done well to have had these words framed and hung in the entrance hall for everyone to see each day when they arrived for class.

When major currencies like the dollar, the euro or the pound sterling are seen to be under threat the banks - the Federal Reserve Bank, the European Central Bank and the Bank of England - usually step in to restore confidence by adjusting interest rates or injecting cash into the economy, a measure that is now euphemistically referred to as 'quantitative easing'. At the same time governments try to encourage investment and promote economic growth by introducing tax incentives. Such measures as these, however, can only ever be stopgap for the underlying causes are not such as can be managed by legislation or decree. It is beyond the remit of politicians and economists to come up with anything other than temporary solutions. This is why the efforts of the German Chancellor and the French President to resolve the euro crisis are proving futile. Since they are not empowered to deal with the underlying causes of the problem, always assuming that they know what they are, they can only ever tinker with the symptoms. The problem of the euro zone is structural and no amount of tinkering can fix it.

Let me round off this consideration of currency and culture by summarising the main points just to make sure that the argument is clear and then let us see where it takes us.

1. For a currency to be credible it must be backed by a culture that is genuinely cohesive, on the one hand, and it must be founded upon sound moral principles, on the other. The euro has failed on both accounts, although not disastrously so. It was a brave attempt but one that was destined to fail. In 2010 the IMF published a paper proposing the adoption of a global currency called the 'bancor' to replace the US dollar as an international reserve currency. Again it is a brave idea but one whose time has not yet come. As things stand right now the bancor would have failed for the same reasons that the euro is about to fail.

2. The only thing that has the capacity to create the 'full fiscal union' that is needed for the euro or any currency to succeed is religion. Just how this might come about we will consider in a later chapter.

3. All is not lost, however, because individual currencies like the American dollar and the British pound can only survive on their own for a while longer. Sooner or later they will recognise the need to become part of a larger monetary unit and when they do the imperative to come up with a credible currency will be rendered all the more urgent and compelling.

4. The idea of the euro is sound in principle; we just do not yet have the means to get there, but we will do one day because this is the only way that humanity can go. Its final destiny is to share a single world economy and this implies that there will be a single currency to go with it, and this will take place just as soon as we have all our moral ducks in line.

All the while that our economy has been falling apart at the seams our planet has been groaning under the strain of the unrelenting demands that are being made upon its resources and it is now telling us that a consumption-led economic model is not sustainable. If Asia with its four billion inhabitants tries to follow the American and European economic model the environment will give out completely. We will rapidly deplete our non-renewable resources and we will terminally pollute our land, air and seas. In short, at the present time there is no economic model on the table that works.

The answer is to be found in self-transformation rather than in the search for a new form of economic governance. The generation of wealth for personal gain must be downgraded in importance and priority must be given to the common good. Our collective welfare must take precedence over individual freedom. Now this may be a hard pill to swallow given that we have been consistently lectured over the years about how indispensable freedom is to human happiness. Be that as it may, we are going to have to understand that freedom is no longer the panacea that we once thought it was. This same freedom that we have rightly fought and died for will, if abused, lead to our downfall. The temple of Apollo at Delphi bore the inscription *'nothing to excess'* and we would have done well to heed its warning. As it is, our obsession with the notion of freedom is taking us ever closer to the condition of the animal.

We are going to have to become less self-centred and more compassionate, less materialistic and more spiritual. And who is going to take the lead in this transformation - Politicians? Economists? Environmentalists? Psychologists? Religionists? No, it is only we, the people, who can bring this change about – the masses, that is, and for this to happen we as individuals must commit to becoming a new race of people, all of us from one end of the planet to the other, in full recognition of the fact that there is only one race of people living on this earth, that we are all dependent upon each other, and that each one of us is precious.

As a species we are fast approaching the stage where we understand that our society, like the individual, and like our planet, is a living organism every atom of which is dependent upon the whole and vice-versa. We await the birth of this new race of men and women as a sine qua non for our survival, both physical and economic. How we are to achieve this regeneration constitutes the raison d'être of this book and we will come to it shortly.

Chapter Twelve

A WORST CASE SCENARIO

Whenever I am invited to speak about my experiences of working in conflict zones in Africa I choose to show a picture of a distraught young woman who looks pregnant and has a child on her back fleeing the burning wreckage of her village in the eastern Democratic Republic of Congo. I found the photo on the internet and whoever was responsible for taking it I thank him or her from the depths of my heart for it captures perfectly the precise moment when life as we know it with a home and a family and a livelihood has been taken from us and we are forced to run for safety, usually heading in whatever direction we happen to be facing at the time.

Those who are fortunate enough to have received advanced warning will have gathered up their children and whatever possessions they can carry - a cooking pot, a plastic jerry can and a mattress being the favourites - and headed for the home of a relative a safe distance away or to an established refugee camp. This is if they are fortunate. If they are not so fortunate then panic will take over. I recall a Liberian refugee with whom I worked in Guinea telling me of his escape from his village when Charles Taylor's men descended upon it killing, raping, looting and torching all at once. He described how he was preparing dinner at the time and was in the middle of plucking a chicken when the rebels appeared. He told me how he ran ten miles before he realised that he still held the chicken in his hand.

Stories like this are not apocryphal they are real and they become everyday events when society breaks down and you quickly learn what is important in life when it does. Let us follow the path of the 'not so fortunate' for a moment to see what likely follows.

Having escaped by the skin of your teeth from certain death you now have to spend the first night out in the open still in a state of panic from your ordeal and now terrified of being attacked by wild animals. After several days on the run with your family in tow you eventually reach somewhere that you hope is safe, probably a rough piece of ground still out in the bush with some insanitary water nearby where others have already settled and you set about installing yourself in close proximity.

The first thing you will need is shelter and so you erect a small trellis of twigs and branches in the shape of a tunnel and you cover it with grass. This is now home for yourself and your family. Very soon you will need to eat. If you happen to have a cooking pot and some flour you can cook up some porridge. If not then you will have to 'borrow' from somewhere. You may be lucky and find yourself near someone who is willing to share what they have, otherwise you will have to go asking around and this is a precarious business, especially for a woman because there is often a price to pay for favours. And you will need three stones to rest your cooking pot on, some firewood and some kindling all of which you may be able to find locally. Meagre though it is, it is a place of your own and you are probably safe for the moment.

What happens next can vary. Let us take the most optimistic scenario and assume that the United Nations High Commission for Refugees (UNHCR) is quick to mobilise and moves in to help after just a few weeks and that nongovernmental organisations are quick to follow, the ones that are equipped to deal with emergencies and specialise in digging latrines, supplying water and setting up clinics. The UNHCR will supply tarpaulins so that you can cover your primitive shelter and protect yourself from the rain, as well as other 'non food items' (NFI's) such as cooking utensils, plastic sheets, mattresses, blankets, mosquito nets, hygiene kits and water containers. The

World Food Programme will commence the distribution of basic food rations that will consist of flour, beans and cooking oil. With this you have the means of survival. Many will be giving profuse thanks to God at this point.

Little by little your basic needs will be met. People will continue to arrive and a community will form perhaps of several hundred or several thousand, or even many thousands. The original dwellings of twigs and straw will be replaced by tents that UNHCR will provide and these may later be replaced by more permanent structures like the traditional African huts with mud walls and thatched roofs that the residents will build themselves. Schools and permanent clinics may be built and UN police may patrol the area to ensure safety. Such were the refugee camps where I first went to work in Guinea's Forest Region. The residents were relatively fortunate and their most common request, that we were never able to grant and which still haunts me to this day, was for a supply of Maggi stock cubes to improve the monotonous taste of the beans and maize-meal that was their daily diet. I deeply regretted not being able to respond to their request but when you are talking of half a million refugees and a possible demand of one hundred thousand Maggi cubes every day, something that is not considered a basic necessity, it was not easy to find a donor.

Of course it is quite possible that none of these things will take place and that the refugees and the internally displaced people, the IDPs, will receive no help from anyone and that they will be left to fend for themselves for months on end, hungry and traumatised, wretched and miserable beyond imagination, and easy prey to anyone of a rapacious bent who will be watching their every move like a hyena on the prowl. This also happens. Some will die, their resistance to disease undermined by intestinal infections and malnutrition.

Perhaps in some people's minds such scenes as these belong exclusively to parts of Africa and could never happen in Britain. They were common enough in Europe during the last century, however, when two World Wars were being fought and hundreds of thousands were displaced and forced to survive as best they could with many scavenging for food wherever they could find it and some dying of hunger. Neither could the liberating armies be relied upon to conduct themselves in a civilised manner. The urgency which defeated Germans sought to surrender to the Americans and the British as opposed to the Soviets is adequate proof.

Human beings everywhere behave in much the same way when the forces of law and order break down. The animal comes unashamedly to the fore and our most primitive instincts are unleashed. People barricade themselves inside their homes too afraid to venture out until their desperation for food exceeds their fear. They arm themselves with whatever weapons they can lay their hands on and prepare to fight to the last. Since the economic crisis began in 2008 the sale of firearms in the United Sates has tripled. Even allowing for the fact that Americans have a love-affair with guns and that the United States is a more violent and materialistic culture than Europe, and also has a higher crime rate, the tendency is clear and it is one that we may expect to see replicated in Britain.

What might precipitate such behaviour? In Britain the process of decline is especially perilous because two separate forces are at work at one and the same time – the decline that necessarily follows empire and the decline that accompanies spiritual decay. Chapter Nine charted the possible stages that our decline may take. We are already dangerously close to the chaos and confusion that it describes and this is even before there has been a major disruption of the economy. If and when our economy does finally collapse the effect will be catastrophic and I sometimes wonder how many of my fellow citizens understand what the implications might be. Let us take a look at some of them.

We have already seen that money itself has no intrinsic value and that when the people who use it cease to believe in it it becomes worthless. The foundation of our currency's stability has been undermined by malfeasance in the finance sector and the confidence that previously upheld it and gave it its worth has been seriously eroded. Frantic efforts are being made to boost the European economy by pumping money into it but no-one knows if it will work. The confidence on which our modern economies depend is fragile and elusive and there is no consensus amongst politicians and economists as to what constitutes it or how it might be recovered. Given the absolutely vital role that confidence plays in world economics it seems remarkable now that we should have taken it for granted for so long and treated it with such irreverence.

When an economy collapses it means that people's savings are wiped out overnight as I have seen in South America on several occasions. It also means that governments will lack the resources to pay for basic services like water and electricity, health, transport and security. Police morale and integrity will vanish in a matter of weeks, if not days. The payment of pensions, both private and state, will be suspended. The army, if it can be mustered in sufficient numbers, will be inadequate to control the rising tide of violent crime. Those who have always supplied our food and other necessities will be unwilling to sell their products because our money is now worthless. So where do people turn for financial security in the absence of a credible currency? Most likely to precious metals like gold and silver and other minerals like diamonds but these are only good to a point because when you hit rock bottom you cannot actually eat them. Food is our bottom line without which we cannot survive; we can make do with just about everything except food. Food that has a long shelf life may well become our currency.

For myself, having spent many years trying to help the farmers and village-dwellers of the developing world, the prices of whose produce has more often than not been set by others who do not actually produce anything, I find a fitting irony in the knowledge that these 'peasant farmers', as they are often called, will be better equipped to survive a full-scale economic collapse than the city-dwellers who have traditionally exploited them. Please consider for a moment the values of a society that puts a higher premium on the contribution of a fashion model, a pop singer and a film star than that of a farmer who produces our very sustenance and then ask yourself whether such a society merits survival?

When society reaches economic melt-down it is every man for himself and socio-economic Darwinism takes over in which only the fittest will survive. It will be the end of civilisation as we know it. There will be no respect for the law, no justice, no security, no compassion, no milk of human kindness. There will be no schools or universities because the law of the jungle will prevail and in the jungle there are none. Secular humanism that put its faith in the inherent goodness of humankind will be exposed for the empty philosophy that it is as we discover that there is no innate moral compass that can be relied upon to keep us on track.

Think of your worst nightmare and this is what will happen. When the dam breaks the people of Britain will be running scared in whatever direction they happen to be facing at the time and they will be entirely dependent on the mercy of others for their survival, just like the Rwandans, Liberians, Sierra Leoneans, Congolese and all the others whose world has been turned upside down. If they are fortunate they will be settled into tented camps in safe areas and they will receive support from the outside. If they are not, then they will be reduced to scavenging. This is what awaits us if we do not put our house in order.

All the horrendous things that we have seen and heard about in Stalinist Russia, Nazi Germany, sub Saharan Africa, Cambodia, the Balkans, you name it, can happen in Britain because the British are no different from anyone else. The only thing that has prevented our descent into similar chaos in the past has been our adherence to the tenets of divine religion which in our case is Christianity. Our stability and our prosperity have been entirely due to the many people who took the teachings of Christ to heart and strove to put them into daily practice. It is to all such people that we have owed our position of pre-eminence and privilege in the world until now. But this spiritual power cannot be counted upon to serve us still because it is no longer present in sufficient quantity to make a difference. Now that we have opted for the material path we can only expect the worst.

This, then, is the nightmare scenario. Does it have to be like this? No, it does not. Nothing has to be anything that we do not want it to be. We have been given free-will and it is ours to exercise as we see fit. There is still time, although we do not know how much exactly, and while there is time there is hope. But this is what can and will happen if people of conscience refuse to act. And sitting on the fence is not an option either. All that has ever been needed for evil to triumph is for good men and women to do nothing. Britain is teetering on the edge of an abyss deeper than any it has ever known and the fact that we are not alone and that the rest of the world is about to follow should be of no consolation.

All the elements of our present crisis have, I trust, been made clear in this book. It is now up to those who understand their import and are moved to take up the fight, to do so. We should be grateful for this opportunity to prove our worth for such an opportunity only comes along very rarely. But this window may not be open to us for much longer. It may soon be shut and our chance to turn things around taken from us.

These words as I write them now are not a wake-up call – it is much too late for this. They are an alarm siren that is summoning every man and woman to the pumps - to pump out the fetid water of our present and to pump back in the crystalline water of our future. Can this really be done and in time? Yes it can. Anything is possible if we go about it in the right way and the right way means that we commit ourselves whole-heartedly and unsparingly to the task in hand, every single one of us, as of this moment. Just what this 'task' consists of constitutes the subject of the second and final part of the book - A Solution.

Young mother fleeing the burning wreckage of her village
in the Eastern Democratic Republic of the Congo

Displaced people on the move in the Eastern Democratic Republic of the Congo

Displaced people en masse in the Eastern Democratic Republic of the Congo

Displaced people's makeshift camp in
the Eastern Democratic Republic of the Congo

PART II

A SOLUTION

Chapter Thirteen

THE TRANSFORMATIVE POWER OF RELIGION

As a matter of urgency we need to find a way to turn things around and get out of the mess that we are in. Fortunately there is a way although it may not be to everyone's liking to hear about it. Please do not think for one moment that I am not aware of the negative reaction that some of the things I am about to say may provoke because I am. And please do not think either that I necessarily enjoy using words like 'spirituality' and 'morality' because I do not. I am as much a part of British culture as anyone in this country and I know only too well that we do not use such terms lightly, nor do we like being preached at. The fact of the matter is that I have tried not to use such terms, and not to speak of religion either, but to no avail. The problem lies not in the words themselves but in the connotations they have acquired over the years. It is as if they are now associated with people who do not live in the real world and have never really suffered, when historically speaking nothing could be further from the truth. I would dearly love not to have to use them but it is simply not possible to do otherwise. And so I will continue in the same vein, always trying to find ways to explain how the invisible impacts the visible without offending too many people in the process.

I would like us now to consider the nature of spiritual transformation and how it affects us, first collectively and then individually. The matter is important because our ability to extricate ourselves from our present predicament depends upon our understanding of the forces involved. We shall need to back-track a little first.

We have seen how the message of Prophet Mohammed radically transformed the peoples of Arabia from a race of barbarians into one of the highest cultures the world has ever seen; how belligerent, impecunious desert nomads became the founders of a peaceful and harmonious civilisation that was to become the envy of the world for its science and technology, its architecture and medicine, and even for its jurisprudence, and how it lay the foundation for other civilisations also, including that of Europe.

Prophet Mohammed was not personally responsible for any of the major advances that took place in the arts and sciences. What he did was to release the creative energy that is present in the Holy Word into the lives of the believers in a way that transformed them into a new race of beings - individuals, that is, who became the building blocks of a new and brilliant civilisation. All the advances in the arts and sciences were subsequent to and dependent upon this massive outpouring of divine spirit that only a messenger of God can bring. To argue along the lines of conventional logic that Arabia was suddenly lucky enough to find itself with a handful of geniuses who came up with inventions and insights that changed the way people thought and acted is unconvincing to say the least.

This outpouring of creative energy brings new potential not only to the arts and sciences but also to the realm of human relations which become characterised by harmony and unity instead of conflict and division. The most enlightened civilisations have all drawn their inspiration from this same Source from the earliest times as we see in the records of Ancient Mesopotamia, the Nile Delta and the Indus Valley. The Americas have had their own messengers of God whose teachings also gave rise to great civilisations whose traditions still survive in part today. We know that ancient Greek philosophers travelled to Judea to consult with Jewish scholars and then returned home with divinely inspired insights and knowledge that transformed their own culture. We know how central justice and compassion were to the teachings of Christ and how insistent he was that we should tend to the needs of the poor, the lame and the sick. Prophet Mohammed introduced a strict code of laws that were designed to protect the poor and defenceless and to give women a status they had not previously known. Such major transformations in our perception and our behaviour do not come about as the result of the endeavours of intellectuals and social reformers. They are the fruits of divine revelation for only such a power as that contained within the Holy Scriptures can truly reshape the hearts and minds of men.

An indication of just how far off course we are in our current thinking concerning the way society moves forward was seen in Time Magazine's choice of Albert Einstein as its 'Man of the Twentieth Century', as if his particular genius had been responsible for shaping the thinking of the human race. The choice smacked of political correctness and felt wrong at the time. The radical changes that have taken place in our consciousness over recent years, the effects of which can be seen all around us, can be traced back well before Einstein appeared on the scene. They can be traced back to the middle of the nineteenth century which is when our new global consciousness with all its dazzling innovation and brilliance found its first tangible expression. We will consider just how this came about in the following chapters. In fact Einstein's theory of relativity is itself now under review and if dethroned, as appears it might be, then one might ask where this will leave Time's 'Man of the Century'? The answer is that he will most likely join the ranks of the countless others whose insights have been bettered over the course of time and become a footnote to the page of history. Would it not have been preferable, one might ask, to have chosen someone of outstanding moral courage whose example will continue to inspire through the ages?

We might note in passing a second example of our failure to apprehend the true genesis of social change and this relates to the modern women's movement which did not begin with the emergence of the Suffragettes as is often supposed. Two decades before the Suffragette movement began a Persian woman by the name of Tahirih had the temerity to remove her veil in the presence of a room filled with men, causing one of them to flee her presence in panic and slit his own throat. She was later condemned to death by strangulation by order of the Muslim clergy, an occasion for which she prepared herself by donning a wedding dress as if in readiness to meet her betrothed. Her final words were 'you can kill me as soon as you like but you can never stop the emancipation of women!' Tahirih was clearly correct in what she said because the women's movement has become an unstoppable force, although not in her own country. It has flourished in countries that were open to innovation and change and where the climate of ideas was favourable. No amount of social activism on her part, always assuming that she had been allowed to live a while longer, would have been sufficient to transform the status of women in her native Persia. The symbiosis needed to make it happen was simply not there.

We must always return to the notion that social progress is an organic process in which a critical mass of right-thinking, right-believing and right-acting people work together in harmony and unison to transform their environment. Their inspiration derives from divine religion and their direction derives from the realisation, as noted in Chapter Eight, that their existence is governed by fixed and reliable scientific laws as ordained by a Law-maker. These two elements taken together would appear to provide us with an infallible road map to the future but it does not always work like this. Things can and do fall apart as we saw in Chapter Nine, *Society in Decline*, and they start to fall apart when we as individuals choose to abandon the path of right living. We have also noted that there is an essential relationship between the worth of a currency and the worth of the people who own it and that when the latter declines the former declines along with it. Now we will consider how deviant behaviour affects material progress and we will take as an example how the highly evolved cultures of pre-Colombian America failed to achieve their full creative potential.

It has always been understood, at least by Europeans, that the wheel is the greatest of inventions and the assumption is that at some point in pre-recorded history some genius perceived the principle and converted it into practical reality and thereafter humanity rolled along nicely and never looked back. The true genius of the invention lies in the fact that there was nothing in nature to copy it from so that the wheel is among the first expressions of humankind's unique capacity to think in abstract that we noted in Chapter Two. This, however, cannot be the whole story. When it comes to technical innovation having a bright idea is not necessarily the most important thing.

We know from pre-Colombian America, for example, that the wheel existed in children's toys so the principle of the wheel was present while the technology was absent. This was despite the existence of enormous empires with extensive trading networks in both Central and South America that would have undoubtedly benefitted from the presence of the wheel. It is true that Native America had no draft animals that might have been used to pull wheeled vehicles, no oxen or cattle or horses for example; in fact they had no beasts of burden at all apart from the weak and temperamental llama that could never be relied upon to do very much, but the wheel could have been used in handcarts if nothing else.

There existed throughout the Inca Empire an impressive system of roads the traces of which can still be seen in places and so one might presume that handcarts would have been useful at the very least for moving agricultural produce around, just as they are in many places of the world today. Then there is the still unresolved issue of how

Native Americans managed to move giant megaliths weighing several tons over long distances, a feat that might conceivably have been made easier had the option of wheeled transport been available. Still today the sight of Native Americans strapping enormous loads to their backs and carrying them long distances on foot is commonplace in the Central Andes, illustrating that old habits die hard.

We need to try to understand how an invention that has been so crucial to our own development might not have been adopted in the Americas. This question is important because both South and Central America had acquired advanced technical expertise in certain fields like architecture, land use and water control, while the latter had reached unsurpassed heights in mathematics and astronomy so that the absence of a technology as simple and as obviously beneficial as the wheel is something of a puzzle, especially when we know that the principle was already present in another form.

We noted in Chapter Eight that when conditions are right technical innovation occurs spontaneously in accordance with need, as it has done in Europe with the telegraph evolving to meet the need to communicate over long distances and the computer evolving to meet the need to process large quantities of information rapidly, and so forth. Given what appear to be the favourable conditions that prevailed in pre-Colombian America one might have expected the technology of the wheel to have evolved in a similarly spontaneous fashion. And yet it did not do so. It is difficult to convey the magnitude of such an omission in cultural terms because there is nothing comparable in our own society – at least nothing that we know of. The most we can do is to try to imagine how something like the space programme, for example, might have fared in the absence of computers. The short answer is that life would have been rendered considerably more difficult.

Successful technological advancement, as we have previously noted, presupposes a coming together of a number of favourable elements. The first and foremost of these is that the hearts and minds of a significant number of men and women have been rendered receptive to the need for change and this condition arrives simultaneously with the adoption of divine religion. Thereafter the determining factors are a fortuitous combination of time, place and personality and this is where the genius of the inventor and the social reformer come in. Their particular insight which is shaped by their environment provides the tangible means for society to move forward. The whole process presupposes an environment that is characterised by a healthy spirit of enquiry and its inventions will appear as its fruit.

Given this, we might conclude that pre-Columbian America, though originally founded on divinely inspired principles, had chosen to abandon the path of right living and thereby squandered its creative potential so that by the time the concept of the wheel came along what might have been a revolutionary technology turned out to be a seed fallen on barren land. Certainly, the early accounts of the Conquistadors who found both empires, especially Central America with its insatiable thirst for human sacrifice, in steep decline when they arrived would seem to bear this out. The Conquistadors, who were just a few hundred in number, systematically crushed the once mighty Aztec and Inca empires like rotten fruit and brought the curtain abruptly down on a morally bankrupt civilisation that was going nowhere, its terminal weakness being ample proof of its advanced state of decay.

We may summarise the nature of collective transformation as follows: it should be seen that everything that has allowed us to progress from one level of existence to the next is the product of divine religion. Every discovery in the sciences, every development in the arts and crafts, and every advance in human relations is the fruit of the new potential that the messenger of God brings to the world and this new potential becomes available to us once a significant critical mass of right-thinking, right-believing and right-acting members of society has been reached. We have all, whether we know it or not, been impelled by this same miraculous force. At the same time it must be understood that this miraculous force is a precious gift that can be easily squandered and that we must strive to protect and preserve it at all costs, and this we do by adhering to the path of right living. Our collective well-being depends upon our so doing.

Now let us consider how spiritual transformation may affect an individual. We have already heard about the notorious slaver John Newton, the same who composed the hymn Amazing Grace, who was involved in the transportation of thousands of innocent men, women and children in the most inhumane conditions from the coasts of Africa to the Americas and how his life was completely turned around by the divine spirit. I will make mention now of another rogue with African connections, this time a Liberian general who fought on behalf of Charles Taylor in the Liberian war of 1989 to 1996. He went by the name of General Butt Naked on account of the fact that he always went into battle wearing only a pair of desert boots and carrying an AK 47. By his own admission he killed twenty thousand of his fellow Liberians.

General Butt Naked killed, maimed and raped at will. I was working in Guinea at the time and saw for myself the wretched state of the refugees as they arrived in tides from Liberia and I learned from them something of the atrocities that were being committed, although not too many, it must be said, were willing to talk about their experiences in any depth. Not that I heard about General Butt Naked himself but I can imagine the kind of things that he did. There seemed to be little pattern to any of the violence.

The story went that Charles Taylor, an Americo-Liberian, meaning one who is descended from the Liberians who returned from America to West Africa after slavery was abolished in the United States in 1865, mysteriously escaped from a Boston prison where he had been sentenced for drug trafficking and made his way back to Liberia. There he put together a small band of rebel fighters whom he had trained in Libya and then overthrew the regime of native Liberian President Samuel Doe which was renowned for its corruption and brutality. It is only now emerging that Charles Taylor had links with the Central Intelligence Agency while he was in prison in Boston, thereby adding to the speculation that has always been around that the CIA facilitated his escape and backed his coup against President Samuel Doe, all of which, if proven, makes the CIA complicit in the carnage and destruction that befell Liberia during its war years.

General Butt Naked served with Charles Taylor's forces although from what I can gather it made little difference which side he was actually on because he seems to have enjoyed killing, maiming and raping for the sake of it. The image of this naked savage on the rampage does not quickly fade. He always claimed, incidentally, that he was protected by magical powers and I suspect that he may well be right in this regard because something must have kept the paparazzi away. A few years ago while imprisoned in a Monrovia gaol he was visited by a Liberian pastor who converted him to Christianity. General Butt Naked, who is now himself a church pastor, has given up his old ways and is now a reformed character who spends his time trying to help people less fortunate than himself, as well as seeking forgiveness from the people he maimed and the relatives of those he killed. I watched a longish documentary on General Butt Naked with the camera following him around even when he thought that he was alone. From what I could tell his conversion appears to be genuine and his repentance heart-felt.

How can one begin to understand how a God of justice could ever begin to forgive the likes of John Newton and General Butt Naked? Assuming that their conversion to Christianity was genuine, and in the case of John Newton we know that it was, we might possibly arrive at a calculation whereby the number of people that John Newton saved from slavery through his political intervention after his conversion to Christianity might somehow equate or even surpass the number whose transportation to the Americas he had contrived. Absurdly hypothetical, no doubt, but there is just a chance that the case for the defence might not be thrown instantly out of court.

In the case of General Butt Naked, however, although I myself might be prepared to accept that his conversion is real I would have to conclude that for most others the jury is probably still out. On the surface of it the man appears to be racked with guilt every waking moment, just as John Newton was, and is now straining every nerve to make amends. The visible evidence of his transformation from beast to man of conscience appears to me to be compelling. As for divine forgiveness there is no way that mere mortals like ourselves can even begin to imagine how such a thing might be possible. Still, as we are told to 'judge not that ye be not judged' we had better refrain from so doing.

What I can say, and it is something that life has taught me, is that behind every success story there is a decision that involves an act of courage and that courage itself is derived from the unknowing – it involves taking a step into the dark. This is the starting point for any radical transformation of our lives and anyone contemplating casting the first stone needs first to consider this. There is also a thought at the back of my mind that there may be a relationship between our capacity for doing good and our capacity for doing evil so that someone who is capable of committing great evil may also be capable of doing great good. The proportions may turn out to be the same so that in the end it becomes a question of where the greatness is directed and to what effect.

Be that as it may, I am glad that I do not have a similar burden on my own conscience. What I do have is sufficient without having the deaths of twenty thousand people and a trail of mayhem to contend with as well. Forgiveness of oneself, as I have discovered at some cost, is far from straight forward. It is something that has to be worked at constantly, and ultimately, I now believe, has to be granted from above. John Newton never managed it and from what I could gather from the documentary General Butt Naked has not managed it either, which may be just as well because I suspect that if he professed to having been forgiven it might well remove his last line of defence. Nonetheless John Newton and General Butt Naked in their later years proved to be of infinitely greater value to the human race than they were in their prime and for this thanks must go to the divine spirit for turning them around, thereby proving that there is no such thing as a truly hopeless case, which must surely come as a consolation to a good many of us.

Chapter Fourteen

A DIVINE SLEIGHT OF HAND

This world of ours can and will be a beautiful place and it may not take us long to get there. The notion has already been put forward that in the future there will be a single economy with a single currency for the whole world and that this will come about just as soon as we get all our moral ducks in line. By 'ducks' is meant two things. The *first duck* is that we recognise our essential interdependence as a species which acknowledges that we only have a limited number of resources at our disposal and that these must be shared equitably. It is not acceptable for one group of people to exploit them mercilessly for their own enrichment and much less is it acceptable to do so at the expense of the health and wellbeing of another group of people. The *second duck* is that we learn to subjugate the promptings of our lower nature and develop to an advanced degree those qualities that belong exclusively to our higher nature, such as compassion, kindness, courtesy, generosity, honesty, truthfulness, trustworthiness, justice, in fact all the virtues that we have always been told to aspire to but seldom did. Nevertheless there will come a time, of this I am certain, when such qualities will be the norm and the waywardness that we see all around us today will be no more than a distant dream.

Once these *two ducks* are properly in line and we have reached this lofty station - and we must if we are to survive - a glorious panorama will open up before us that we might expect to look something like this:

The qualified peace between nations that we have already noted is present in our emerging world order will fully mature and a golden age of lasting peace will be ushered in.

There will be elected by universal suffrage a government that will represent the interests of the entire world.

Our future society will almost certainly not carry a political label but if it did it would be something like 'theocratic socialism'. The rule of law that will apply to everyone with no loopholes for the rich and famous will be based on divinely inspired principles. The interdependence of capital and labour will be recognised and the extremes of wealth and poverty will be eliminated. Education and health care will be available and affordable for all. It will be a society in which the rights and the responsibilities of the individual are recognised and work will be elevated to the station of worship. Individual initiative and endeavour will be rewarded, while sloth will be condemned.

Our society will be largely self-regulating. There will be a police force for the purpose of maintaining order but it is doubtful that it will have much to do. The weapons industry will become all but defunct, just producing limited numbers of firearms for the police to use in the unlikely event that they are needed to maintain internal control.

There will be a universal auxiliary language that we will all learn from birth so that anyone will be able to travel to any corner of the world and converse with those who live there as if he were in his own country. There will be no need for passports because there will be no borders. Countries will still exist and so will national identities but without any notions of superiority or exclusivity. There will be no barriers between them and people will be free to take their skills and go and work wherever they choose, no questions asked. Prejudice will have effectively disappeared leaving no trace of the divisions of race and class that have so bedevilled our world. Unity in diversity will be our guiding light.

Far-fetched, you may think, but most of the conditions needed for this heaven on earth to take place are already with us. The revolution in consciousness that attained its first expression in the mid nineteenth century has been pushing us forward in this direction at an ever accelerating pace. A profusion of institutions has already emerged to address issues of finance, health, education, security, human rights and climate change that affect us all illustrating that an awareness of a need for global governance is well established.

A genuine world community could not function without the requisite infrastructure and we now have it. If we stop to consider that a letter sent by the Royal Geographical Society in London to Dr. David Livingstone in Central Africa in the mid nineteenth century would have gone by sea and land and taken several months to get there and that today anyone who can afford the airfare could deliver the same message by hand in about twelve hours, it beggars belief. Better still, anyone with a mobile phone can deliver the same message in a matter of seconds. We now have a communications network that spans the globe in a fashion that would have been unimaginable just a century ago and which even the most sceptical among us has to admit has made the world a better place. All such inventions have had the effect of reinforcing our connectedness yet none of them were specifically designed for this purpose.

Those who have led the process of technical innovation, namely the scientists and the engineers, were themselves unaware of the direction that their efforts were taking them. Occasionally someone would ask a question like, 'does the presence of the internet now mean that governments can no longer apply censorship?'; or 'does the invention of the mobile phone mean that landlines will soon become obsolete?'; or 'does the existence of social networks mean that culture is changing faster?' But it is always a game of 'catch-up' as we strive to understand where the latest innovation is taking us. It is always a question of where is *it* taking *us*, and never a question of where are *we* taking *it*. At no point have we been fully in charge.

The unqualified peace and stability that we are eventually to enjoy will not come about as a result of sustained economic growth no matter how widespread, nor will it be the product of peace agreements signed between governments. It will be the result of a personal choice taken by individuals on a universal scale to curb their lower instincts and aspire to a higher set of principles. This and this alone can guarantee lasting peace. At the same time it will be reinforced by a vision and a purpose that will be shared by everyone.

The peace that we are experiencing at the present time may be described as a 'lesser peace' in the sense that it has been imposed upon us. This 'lesser peace' will eventually give way to a 'greater peace' at a time when we are properly prepared and ready and it will be instituted by ourselves. It will represent a conscious choice on our part to reconnect with our Creator. The arrival of the 'greater peace' will be the sign of mankind's coming of age. It will be seen as the culmination of a process which parallels our expanding social consciousness and which has seen us pass through the stages of birth, infancy and adolescence to maturity. It will represent the fulfilment of human potential and the coming of the Kingdom of God on Earth.

Three primary forces are combining to reveal to us the true extent of our interconnectedness and bring us closer together. The first is the revolution in communications technology just mentioned; the second is our economic crisis which we now understand cannot be solved by any nation in isolation; and the third is the environment the degradation of which affects us all. An analogy might be three sheepdogs driving sheep into a pen: the three sheepdogs represent the three forces just mentioned; the sheep are the human race; and the pen is the global community. There is no escape from this process because ultimately there can be no survival outside the pen of a united world. This means that we either acquire the virtues needed to live together in harmony or we fight each other to the death, and the latter, as we have already noted, is an option that is becoming less available to us by the day. Another term for describing what we are currently going through is 'Judgement Day'.

Needless to say there will be a great many who reject such a vision out of hand as being hopelessly Utopian and this is to be expected; nothing of any value can come about without a struggle. We have seen what I am referring to as a 'lesser peace' emerge from the darkness of impossibility only after a painful and protracted struggle that took most of the twentieth century to gather momentum. Its first tangible expression was seen in the League of Nations which emerged as a faint candle of hope in 1919 amid the rubble of the First World War and which later gave way to the United Nations whose existence, flawed though it often is, few of us would now question. Thereafter we have seen the emergence of an alphabet soup of regional groupings, EU, ASEAN, SADEC, NAFTA, MERCOSUR, COMESA, ECOWAS, APEC and so forth, all of them concerned with promoting peaceful cooperation between their members.

The idealism on which such initiatives have been founded was often ridiculed as being hopelessly irrelevant to an age that was characterised by the most destructive conflicts the world has ever seen. Nonetheless a momentum for peace took hold so that by the end of the century it had, against all conceivable odds, become virtually unthinkable for one nation to invade another. Conflict still exists, of course, but it is of a different kind in which ideology across borders is taking the place of national interests, which is also regrettable but is not without its compensations. On the one hand it represents a shift away from the blinkered nationalism that corrupted so much of our thinking in the twentieth century to an assertion of individual belief; and on the other it indicates that a search for a meaning to life is taking precedence over material gain. Nevertheless it is perfectly evident that the causes that such ideologues espouse, backed as they are by intransigence and violence, are tragically flawed and must sooner or later come to nothing.

The real reason why sovereign states no longer contemplate invading each other is that it no longer seems a sensible thing to do - it is as simple as this - and herein lies the 'divine sleight of hand'. It was not by our own choosing that we arrived at this point – would that it were! It is because a force greater than anything that we ourselves could muster or even imagine chose to intervene and remove this option from us. It represents a decision that was taken on our behalf and without our consent but for which we should be eternally grateful. Swords are being beaten into plough shares, just as foretold. We shall be taking another look at this phenomenon of world peace in the remaining chapters.

Cynicism has been a major obstacle to progress ever since time began and it is not difficult to imagine the voices of detractors in the past decrying the possibility of the integration of the clan into the tribe or the tribe into the nation state, just as we can hear the voices of dissent today decrying the possibility of a united world. Cynicism is no easy matter to deal with for it carries its own logic – the logic of inertia - every cynic being living proof of his own words. Phrases like 'people will never change', and 'evil has always been with us and always will be', come readily to mind and such mindsets are not easily altered. The best way to deal with cynicism, I have found, is to ignore it and to show that there is another way. Actions will always speak louder than words and people usually start to take note when they see they are being left behind. It is not dissimilar to those who protest that 'there is too much suffering in the world for God to exist'. When it is pointed out to them that it is usually those who believe in the existence of God who do most to relieve the suffering the issue takes on a different dimension. There is a truth in action that transcends the logic of debate.

There are so many positive things that are going on in the world right now that it is difficult for cynicism to retain its hold. The arrival of the lesser peace is one of them; a universal concern for human rights is another; and a growing concern for economic and social justice is another. It is as if humanity, suddenly aware of its new potential, is scrambling to put its house in order. To these we may add some truly marvellous advances in medical science. Who would not be moved by the sight of conjoined twins being successfully separated or the 'blade-runner' Oscar Pistorius in full flow? And then there is the dazzling spectacle of an unfolding universe that space technology is bringing into our own homes! On top of this and seemingly come from out of nowhere is the 'Arab Spring' which is yet another indication that something seismic is going on, illustrating as it does that a blinkered view of the world which denies men and women the right to investigate truth for themselves is no longer tenable. Such events bear the hallmark of a new day.

Slowly but surely the weight of positive experience will prevail and the walls of cynicism will come down. No longer will we hear mention of 'a God conspiracy', or 'religion is the opium of the people,' nor even such semi humorous comments as 'thank God I am an atheist!' Such negativity may still run deep with us yet those who have been around long enough to live through difficult times will know that it need not present an insurmountable obstacle. Sometimes what seems like a cast iron certainty of failure is the prelude to success. It is as if we need to see an obstacle in its awesome entirety before it can be overcome and this we are able to do because of an intuitive awareness of its absence. The converse can also be true, of course, in that just when we think we have finally 'got it made' our world falls apart; the novelist Howard Spring referred to this as 'the sunset touch'. There may not be any scientific basis to this but, like Karl Jung's notion of synchronicity which had no scientific basis to it either but is now accepted as real, it may one day find its way into an encyclopaedia of authentic human experience. I sometimes take refuge in something that former British prime minister, Harold MacMillan, said long after he left office, and it may well turn out to be his one lasting contribution to our collective wisdom – 'when the generality of mankind is united on a single issue, it is invariably wrong'.

Be that as it may, we should expect that the day will soon come when the generality of mankind will have learned the all important lesson that a society without religion falls into chaos and confusion and we will have reinstated religion in its rightful place at the centre of our lives. All that is required is for us sorry creatures called human beings to understand that we are at one with each other and to remove the barriers that keep us apart, and all of these barriers, just in case anyone needs reminding, are to be found in our lower nature.

Chapter Fifteen

PROPHECY

It is mentioned in all the world's religions that in the fullness of time a great spiritual teacher will appear and that he will sort out the mess that we have made. He has been referred to in a number of ways and amongst them are the following: the return of Krishna (Hinduism); the Lord of Hosts (Judaism); the Lord of the Age (Zoroastrianism); the Metteyya or Fifth Buddha (Buddhism); the Spirit of Truth and the Return of Christ (Christianity); and the Mahdi, the Spirit of Jesus Christ and the Twelfth Imam (Islam). The precise manner of his return and what he will do when he gets here has been a matter of serious debate within the respective traditions but the one thing that they are all agreed upon is that a great spiritual teacher will appear and that he will dispense justice. Christians, for example, for two thousand years have been saying the following prayer: 'Thy Kingdom come, Thy will be done on earth as it is in heaven' and the expectation is that Christ will return to the earth to judge humanity and bring order to chaos.

What I would like to do now is to look at just a small handful of the many prophecies as they appear in their respective traditions and then, in the remaining chapters, consider how they relate to what is happening in our world right now. The oldest tradition that we know of is Hinduism so let us start here.

Hinduism

In the Bhagavad Gita (4:7-8) Lord Krishna says:

'Whenever there is a decline in righteousness, O Bharat, and the rise of irreligion, it is then that I send forth My spirit.

For the salvation of the good, the destruction of the evil-doers, and for firmly establishing righteousness, I manifest myself from age to age'.

Hindus are awaiting the return of Krishna or one they refer to as the Kalki Avatar and his appearance will mark the end of the Kali Yuga (Dark or Iron Age) and the beginning of a Sat or Krta Yuga (Golden Age). The Kali Yuga is described in such terms as:

'In the Kali Yuga wealth alone will be the deciding factor of nobility and brute force will be the only standard in establishing or deciding what is righteous or not.

Mutual liking will be the deciding factor in choosing a partner in marriage; cheating will be the order of the day in business relations; satisfaction of sexual pleasure will be the only consideration of male or female excellence and worthiness; and the wearing of the sacred thread (Yajnopavita) will be the outward index of being a Brahmin'. (Bhagavata Purana).

'When deceit, falsehood, lethargy, sleepiness, violence, despondency, grief, delusion, fear and poverty prevail, that is the Kali Yuga...

Mortal beings will become dull-witted, unlucky, voracious, destitute of wealth but voluptuous, and women wanton and unchaste.

People will have their minds weighed down with constant anxiety and fear. This will be due to devastating famine and heavy taxation. The land will not grow food crops and the people will always be in fear of pending droughts'. (Bhagavata Purana).

Similar prophecies are found in other passages of Hindu Scriptures such as the Ramayana, the Mahabharata and the Vishnu Purana.

'When the Vedic religion and the dharma of the law books have nearly ceased and the Kali Yuga is almost exhausted, then a part of the Creator of the entire universe...the blessed Lord Vasudeva (Vishnu) will become incarnate here in the universe in the form of Kalki'. (Vishnu Purana 4:24, see also Bhagavata Purana XII, 2:16).

Judaism

'The people that walked in darkness have seen a great light; they that dwell in the land of the shadow of death, upon them hath the light shined...For thou hast broken the yoke of his burden, and the staff of his shoulder, the rod of his oppressor, as in the day of Midian. For every battle of the warrior is with confused noise and garments rolled in blood; but this shall be with burning and fuel of fire. For unto us a child is born unto us a son is given; and the government shall be upon his shoulders; and his name shall be called Wonderful, Counsellor, the Mighty God, the Everlasting Father, the Prince of Peace. Of the increase of his government and peace there shall be no end, upon the throne of David, and upon his kingdom, to order it, and to establish it with judgement and with justice from henceforth even forever. The zeal of the Lord of Hosts will perform this' (Isaiah IX 2-7).

This passage has often been taken by Christians to refer to Christ and indeed some of it is perfectly apt in the sense that Christ came as a light and a Saviour to those in darkness. However at no time has the 'government been upon his shoulders'. Furthermore Christ said that he 'came not to bring peace but a sword' and in fact throughout the whole Christian era wars have been common. There is good reason to believe, therefore, that this passage refers not to Christ but to another who will come after him and who will usher in a time of just government and peace.

The prophet Micah relates these days to the return of the Jews to their homeland:

'I will surely assemble, O Jacob, all of thee; I will surely gather the remnant of Israel; I will put them together...as the flock in the midst of their fold' (Micah 2:12)

And he prophesied that:

1. *In the last days it shall come to pass, that the mountain of the house of the Lord shall be*

established in the top of the mountains, and it shall be exalted above the hills, and people shall flow unto it. (Micah IV, 1)

2. *And many nations shall come and say, Come, and let us go up to the mountain of the Lord, and to the house of the God of Jacob.* (Micah IV, 2)

3. *And he shall judge among many people, and rebuke strong nations afar off; and they shall beat their swords into ploughshares, and their spears into pruning hooks; nation shall not lift up sword against nation, neither shall they learn war any more.* (Micah IV,3)

And he also prophesied that:

i) The Promised One would come from the east (Assyria);

ii) From the fortified cities;

iii) From the fortress even to the river;

iv) From sea to sea;

v) From mountain to mountain;

vi) The land (that he came to) would be desolate;

vii) According to the days of thy coming out of the land of Egypt will I show unto him marvellous things. (Micah VI 12,15)

The prophet Ezekiel (43:12) prophesied:

'And the glory of the Lord came into the house by way of the gate whose prospect is toward the east'.

The Prophet Jeremiah:

'And I will set my throne in Elam...' (Jeremiah 49:38)

Zoroastrianism

Zoroastrianism originated in eastern Iran approximately

three thousand years ago. Its founder was named Zarathustra but is better known by the Greek version of Zoroaster. Most Zoroastrians today are located in India in the Bombay area with a minority still living in Iran. Although originally a monotheistic religion Zoroastrianism has become altered over the years and a doctrine of two co-eternal and contesting principles of good and evil have taken centre stage. The sacred writings are known as Avesta or Zend-Avesta, although much of the original scriptures have been lost. Zoroastrians who believe that moral judgement follows death are known for their high ethical standards as summed up in 'good thoughts, good words and good deeds'.

Zoroaster foretold that a period of three thousand years of conflict and contention must precede the advent of the World Saviour Shah-Bahram (Lord of the Age) who would triumph over evil and usher in an era of blessedness and peace.

Buddhism

'I am not the first Buddha who came upon the earth, nor shall I be the last. Previously, there were many Buddhas who appeared in this world. In due time, another Buddha will arise in this world, within this world cycle, a Holy One, a supremely enlightened One...an incomparable Leader of men...He will reveal to you the same eternal truths which I have taught you.' (Chakkavatti Sihanada Suttanta D.III,76).

Gautama Buddha prophesied:

'At that period, brethren, there will arise in the world an Exalted One named Metteyya, Arahat, Fully Awakened, abounding in wisdom and goodness, happy, with knowledge of the worlds, unsurpassed as a guide to mortals willing to be led, a teacher for gods and men, an Exalted One, a Buddha, even as I am now. He, by himself, will thoroughly know and see, as it were face to face, this universe, with its worlds of the spirits, its Brahmas and its Maras, and its world of recluses and Brahmins, of princes

and peoples, even as I now, by myself, thoroughly know and see them'. (Digha Nikaya)

And,

'The truth, lovely in its origin, lovely in its progress, lovely in its consummation, will he (Metteyya Buddha) proclaim, both in the spirit and in the letter; the higher life will he make known, in all its fullness and in all its purity, even as I do now. He will be accompanied by a congregation of some thousands of brethren, even as I am now accompanied by a congregation of some hundreds of brethren.' (Digha Nikaya)

According to Buddhist tradition the Metteyya Buddha will come from the west (i.e. west of India).

With regard to timing, Gautama Buddha said:
'The Buddha Supreme, now am I
But after me Metteyya comes,
Before this auspicious aeon
Runs to the end of its years'. (Anagatavamsa)

Moojan Momen in his book Buddhism and the Baha'i Faith comments:

'This passage clearly shows that the Metteyya Buddha will appear 'before this auspicious aeon runs to the end of its years'. Since Gautama Buddha appeared in India and was speaking to disciples who had been Hindus and were familiar with the Hindu system of dating cycles, it would seem likely that when Gautama Buddha said 'before this auspicious aeon runs to the end of its years', he was speaking of the Hindu Kali Yuga in the middle of which he had appeared. This Kali Yuga ended at noon on 1st August 1943, equivalent of 2486 of the Buddhist Era. Therefore according to this prophecy of the Buddha, the Metteyya Buddha should have appeared sometime before 1943 AD'. (pp. 49-50)

Christianity

'And they shall fall by the edge of the sword, and shall be led away captive into all nations: and Jerusalem shall be trodden down of Gentiles, until the times of the Gentiles be fulfilled...And then shall they see the Son of man coming in a cloud with power and great glory'. (Luke 21: 24-27)

'And this gospel of the kingdom shall be preached in all the world for a witness unto all nations; and then shall the end come'. (Matthew 24:12)

'But the day of the Lord will come as a thief in the night; in which the heavens shall pass away with a great noise, and the elements shall melt with fervent heat, the earth also and the works that are therein shall be burnt up'. (II Peter iii.10)

'Know this first, that there shall come in the last days scoffers, walking after their own lusts, and saying, Where is the promise of his coming? For since the fathers fell asleep, all things continue as from the beginning of the creation.' (Peter 2, 3:3-4)

'This know also, that in the last days perilous times shall come. For men shall be lovers of their own selves, covetous, boasters, proud, blasphemers, disobedient to parents, unthankful, unholy, without natural affection, trucebreakers, false accusers, incontinent, fierce, despisers of those that are good, traitors, heady, high-minded, lovers of pleasures more than lovers of God; Having a form of godliness, but denying the power thereof: from such turn away.' (Timothy 2, 3:1-5)

'I have many things to say unto you, but ye cannot bear them now.

Howbeit when he, the Spirit of Truth, is come, he will guide you into all truth: for he shall not speak of himself; but whatsoever he shall hear, that shall he speak: and he will show you things to come'. (John XVI: 12-13)

Islam

Islam, like the other religions, is not entirely clear concerning the role that the great Spiritual Teacher will play when he gets here. There are no references to his coming in the Koran, nor in the Hadith. The concept of the Mahdi appears to have developed in the second and third centuries of the Muslim era and been passed down as an oral tradition. In Sunni Islam there is a general belief that there will be two figures, one of whom is referred to as the Mahdi ('Guided by God') who will rule for a short period before the Day of Judgement and, together with Jesus, will rid the world of evil. In Shia Islam there is a belief in the appearance of a figure known as the Twelfth Imam who according to tradition went into hiding following the deaths of the previous eleven Imams and will re-appear on the Day of Judgement. There is no absolute clarity as to whether the role of the Twelfth Imam is identical to that of the Mahdi or whether he represents the return of Jesus Christ. At all events this Figure is seen as the Redeemer of Mankind. An Islamic tradition gives the date of 1260A.H. (1844 AD) in the Muslim calendar for the appearance of the Twelfth Imam, that is, one thousand years after his 'disappearance' in 260 A.H.

'Believers, Jews, Zoroastrians and Christians who believe in God and the Judgement Day and who do good works shall surely be rewarded by God'. (Koran 2:62)

'The righteous shall surely dwell in bliss. But the wicked shall burn in Hell-fire upon the Judgment Day: they shall not escape.' (Koran 82:11)

'The world will not come to an end until the Arabs are ruled by a man from my family'. (Sunan Abi Dawud: 11: 370)

'In the time of the Mahdi, a Muslim in the East will be able to see his Muslim brother in the West, and he in the West will see him in the East.' (Bihar al-Anwar: 52: 391)

'Would that you knew what the Day of Judgment is! Oh, would that you knew what the Day of Judgment is! It is the day when every soul will stand alone and Allah will reign supreme.' (Koran 82:11)

'On that day the sky with all its clouds shall be rent asunder and the angels sent down in their ranks. On that day the Merciful will truly reign supreme. A day of woe it shall be to the unbelievers.' (Koran 25:26)

'The Trumpet shall be sounded and all who are in heaven and earth shall fall down fainting, except those that shall be spared by Allah. Then the Trumpet will sound again and they shall rise and gaze around them. The earth will shine with the light of her Lord, and the Book will be laid open. The prophets and witnesses shall be brought in and all shall be judged with fairness: none shall be wronged. Every soul shall be paid back according to its deeds, for Allah knows of all their actions.' (Koran 39:68)

The foregoing tells us that the appearance of a great Spiritual Teacher, or a Messiah, has been prophesied by all the world's religions and that the world will be in a sorry state when he gets here and in dire need of his intervention. The question is, will the world recognise him and listen to what he has to say? In the past we did not do too well in this regard; will we do any better this time? This is a question that only we as individuals can answer. Whether we listen or not is a personal choice that is made on the basis of free will and which no-one can force us to make. It is like the proverbial horse that can be taken to water but cannot be made to drink. The most anyone can do is to remove the obstacles from the seeker's path and to try to make the water attractive enough for him to want to drink, but the final choice will be his. This is what the remaining chapters will try to do, namely, to make the water attractive enough not just for us to drink, but to dive straight in.

Chapter Sixteen

PROPHECY FULFILLED

Prophecy is of two kinds: literal and metaphorical. The former can be understood intellectually and is straight forward while the latter is to be understood spiritually and is intuitive. It is intended that certain prophecies should only be accessible through the spirit because the purpose of religion is to attract those who are sympathetic to the message and this implies commitment. There has to be some merit in achieving what is humankind's ultimate goal. If it were too simple, like solving a child's crossword puzzle, then it would be available to everyone whether they deserve it or not. Needless to say the more deserving we become the more accessible the message becomes also.

Most of the religious leaders at the time of Christ failed to recognise him when he appeared because they adhered literally to prophecies that were meant to be taken metaphorically. The Jews were expecting a Messiah who would, according to their traditions, wield a great sword, sit on a mighty throne and rule over a mighty kingdom. In fact some of a political inclination were expecting their Messiah to lead a successful revolt against the Roman occupation and liberate the Jewish people. When they saw that Jesus Christ did none of these things, nor did he have any interest in doing them, they laughed him to scorn and called him an imposter. Had they had spiritual eyes and ears, however, they would have understood that the 'sword' that Christ wielded was the sword of truth; that the 'throne' that he sat on was the throne of God by Whose authority he ruled; and that his 'empire' was the hearts of men and women which today, two thousand years later, numbers two thousand million souls, in contrast to mighty Rome whose empire disappeared long ago.

In all things spiritual, humility is the key. When it comes to recognising God's messenger I suspect that conditions may not be vastly different today from any time in the past when the more devout believers had their check list for the appearance of their Promised One in hand ready to start ticking the boxes. The same is happening now; the more devout ones among us are gearing up to put the messenger of God to their test. It is my understanding that the Creator does things the other way round; He puts us to His test and we need humility to pass it.

We see amongst fundamentalist Christians today the same tendency to take every word of their scriptures literally just as the Jews did two thousand years ago. As a Brit brought up in a Christian environment that was characterised by moderation and common sense I was more than a little surprised to discover that many evangelical Christians in the United States are expecting Christ to *literally* return on a cloud and for the dead in Christ to *literally* rise up from their graves and meet him in the air. This strikes me as highly unlikely. The metaphorical interpretation seems much more plausible to me, namely, that Christ's return will dispel the clouds of superstition and ignorance that prevent humanity from seeing the sun of truth and will cause those who are spiritually dead to spring into spiritual life. In other words, the 'clouds' and the 'graves' are metaphors for ungodliness and are not to be taken literally. The pure in heart will understand this.

Let us consider some of the prophecies mentioned in the previous chapter and decide whether or not they hold water. At this point in what is the penultimate chapter of the book I feel I need to put all my cards on the table and make clear that the conversion that I underwent at 3am on 14th July 1975 in my room in Liverpool has not undergone any revision. Each day since that time has only served to confirm the authenticity of the religion that I embraced in that moment, the Baha'i Faith. It is my belief that the founder of the Baha'i Faith, whose title is the Glory of God, is none other than the great Spiritual Teacher that the world has been anxiously waiting for and who has come in accordance with prophecy to establish the Kingdom of God on earth.

What we are witnessing right now in the turmoil that is going on around us is the dying of an old order and the birth of a new one. Its origin can be traced back to the middle of the nineteenth century, to the 22nd May 1844 to be exact, when a young Persian merchant named Siyyid Ali Mohammed, a descendant of the Prophet Mohammed, assumed the title of the 'Bab' or 'Gate' and declared that he had come to prepare the way for one who was infinitely greater than himself, this person being none other than the Glory of God, or Baha'u'llah to give him his Arabic title. Baha'u'llah declared his mission as the Promised One of all Ages in a garden just outside the city of Baghdad in April 1863 on the eve of his exile from Baghdad to Constantinople. Let us examine how his claim to be the great Spiritual Teacher that the world has been anxiously waiting for stacks up.

Baha'u'llah claimed to have unsealed the books of which the prophet Daniel spoke. One of the truths that he unsealed is that of progressive revelation which holds that religious truth is relative and evolves in accordance with the needs of an evolving civilisation. He tells us that, *'All men have been created to carry forward an ever-advancing civilisation'*.

At the same time he confirmed that all religions are one in essence and derive from the same Source and that no distinction should be made between them in terms of their intrinsic merit. All the messengers of God are perfect beings who have been empowered to convey the divine word and bring order to the world. Thus he confirms the words of Lord Krishna *'whenever there is a decline in righteousness and a rise in irreligion He (God) sends forth His spirit'*; as well as those of Gautama Buddha who said *'I am not the first Buddha who came upon the earth, nor shall I be the last'*.

We see in these statements the Baha'i concept of 'Return' meaning that God manifests himself, not just once but repeatedly through His divine messengers. In so far as each messenger of God is a perfect being who represents the Creator they are to be considered one and the same even though they are different individuals with different names appearing in different places at different times. The exclusivity that some believers claim for their own particular Faith, therefore, must give way to an acceptance of the oneness of all religion. Far from claiming finality for his revelation Baha'u'llah asserts that other messengers of God with new revelations will follow.

With regard to the *timing* of Baha'u'llah's advent in the mid nineteenth century we should note that:

It is consistent with the three thousand years foretold by Zoroaster.

According to Jewish prophecy the Jews are not supposed to return to their homeland until the Lord of Hosts has appeared which presents a problem for Jewish scholars given that the state of Israel has been in existence since 1948 while the Lord of Hosts, according to them, has yet to appear. In fact the Jews were first permitted to return to their homeland in 1844 when the Turkish Government which at that time governed Palestine as part of the Ottoman Empire, under pressure from Great Britain, issued what is known as the Edict of Toleration.

Buddhist prophecy holds that the Metteyya Buddha will appear before the completion of the Hindu Kali Yuga which occurred in the year 2486 of the Buddhist era or 1943 AD. This date, therefore, is consistent with Baha'i teachings.

Christ gave as a condition for his return 'when the times of the gentiles have been fulfilled' which we have just seen was in 1844. He gave as another condition 'when the Gospel had been preached in all the world for a witness' which was reckoned by a good many 'millennial' scholars who were eagerly preparing for Christ's return to be the middle of the nineteenth century.

Muslim prophecy gave the date of 1260 A.H. or 1844 AD for the appearance of the Mahdi or Twelfth Imam.

The Hadith quote Prophet Mohammed as saying that the world would not come to an end until the Arabs were ruled by a man from his family. Siyyid Ali Mohammad who took the title of the 'Bab' was descended from this holy lineage.

We may conclude, therefore, that the declaration of Siyyid Ali Mohammed on 22nd May 1844 as the one who had come to prepare the way for a new messenger of God was consistent with the prophecies of the major religions.

The *location* of Persia as a place of divine revelation is also consistent with many scriptures. The land of Elam mentioned by the prophet Jeremiah was a part of ancient Persia just as it is part of Iran today. The prophet Daniel was living in the capital city of ancient Persia, Shushan, when he had his vision of the first and second comings of Christ and when he prophesied that Elam would be a place of vision in the latter days. The prophet Ezekiel wrote that *'the glory of the Lord came into the house by way of the gate whose prospect is toward the east'*. Persia is east of Babylon where Ezekiel was residing at the time of his vision. Ezekiel also refers to the 'gate' which is the title taken by the Bab, Baha'u'llah's forerunner. Buddhist tradition says that the Metteyya Buddha will come from the 'west'. Persia is west of India.

The prophet Micah provides us with a remarkable series of prophecies all of them accurately predicting Baha'u'llah's exile as a prisoner from Iran to Iraq, to Turkey and finally to Palestine. Let us look again at what he wrote:

i) *The Promised One would come from the east (Assyria).* The Assyrian empire included the western part of Persia the land where Baha'u'llah was born and Babylon (Iraq) where he declared his mission.

ii)   *From the fortified cities;* Baha'u'llah was exiled from the fortified city of Constantinople to the fortified city of Akka.

iii) *From the fortress even to the river;* When released from prison in Akka Baha'u'llah travelled to an island in the river called Na'matn.

iv)   *From sea to sea;* Baha'u'llah was exiled from the Black Sea to the Mediterranean Sea.

v)   *From mountain to mountain;* Baha'u'llah travelled from Mt. Sar-Galu in Kurdistan (where he withdrew into the wilderness) to Mount Carmel in Palestine.

vi)   *The land (that he came to) would be desolate;* Akka was rife with typhoid, malaria, diphtheria and dysentery. Many of his followers died.

vii) *According to the days of thy coming out of the land of Egypt will I show unto him marvellous things.*

The time of the coming out of Egypt was forty years. Baha'u'llah's ministry lasted from the first intimation of his mission which took place in an underground dungeon in Tehran in August 1852 until his death in May 1892.

Let us look at Micah's other prophecies:

1. *In the last days it shall come to pass, that the mountain of the house of the Lord shall be established in the top of the mountains, and it shall be exalted above the hills, and people shall flow unto it.* (Micah IV, 1).

Today the supreme administrative body of the Baha'i Faith, the Universal house of Justice, is located at the top of Mount Carmel, in Haifa, Israel. Many thousands of Baha'i pilgrims visit Mount Carmel every year.

2. *And many nations shall come and say, Come, and let us go up to the mountain of the Lord, and to the house of the God of Jacob.* (Micah IV, 2).

Increasing numbers of visitors hailing from all over the world visit the Baha'i world centre on Mount Carmel every year, not least to see its magnificent gardens where the 'desert has bloomed'.

3. *And he shall judge among many people, and rebuke strong nations afar off; and they shall beat their swords into ploughshares, and their spears into pruning hooks; nation shall not lift up sword against nation, neither shall they learn war any more.* (Micah IV,3).

In 1868 Baha'u'llah, while a prisoner of the Ottoman Empire, wrote letters announcing his mission to the Sultan of Turkey, the Shah of Persia, the Pope and to many of the crowned heads of Europe including Queen Victoria, Czar Nicolaevitch Alexander II of Russia and French Emperor Napoleon III. In these letters he 'proclaimed himself to be the King of Kings, declared them to be his vassals, bade them forsake their palaces and hasten to gain admittance into his kingdom. He invites these kings to hold fast to the 'Lesser Peace', exhorts them to be reconciled amongst themselves, to unite and reduce their armaments, and bids them to refrain from laying excessive burdens on their subjects'. (God Passes By, Shoghi Effendi).

Baha'u'llah sent a second letter to Emperor Napoleon III, the first one having been 'cast behind his back', prophesying that his kingdom shall be 'thrown into confusion' and that his empire shall 'pass from his hands', and that 'commotions shall seize all the people of that land' unless he arise to help the Cause of God. The Second French Empire was overthrown three days after Napoleon's disastrous surrender and capture at the Battle of Sedan in 1870 which resulted in the proclamation of the French Third Republic and the cession of the territory of Alsace-Lorraine to the newly formed German Empire.

It is the saddest of ironies that the land that has been chosen as the place for God's latest revelation to mankind,

Iran, should have responded with such savagery from the moment of its birth. Since the Bab's declaration on 22nd May 1844 some 20,000 followers of the new religion have been killed and many thousands of others tortured, imprisoned and exiled. The Bab himself was executed by firing squad in the town of Tabriz in 1850, while Baha'u'llah, himself a nobleman, was first imprisoned and then exiled from Tehran to Bagdad in 1853; then exiled again to Constantinople and Adrianople in 1863; and then exiled again in 1868 to the prison city of Akka where he passed away in 1892. Many of his followers, both men and women, are languishing in Iranian prisons at the present time. And as if to provide us with the ultimate of all ironies the Iranian president, while lamenting the current state of the world, recently proclaimed, 'Oh, how I long for the Mahdi to come!'

On what grounds are Baha'is persecuted in Iran? In actual fact there are none. The Baha'i Faith fully accepts the divine authority of Prophet Mohammed and the Koran so the question of apostasy is not an issue. The problem lies in a single line in the Koran which certain Muslims have interpreted to mean that Mohammed is the last prophet and that there can be no prophet after him so that anyone claiming such a station must, by definition, be a false prophet. The line in question is:

'Mohammed is the Father of no man and the Seal of the Prophets'. (Koran 33:40)

The first part is correct in that Prophet Mohammed had two sons both of whom died leaving him with four daughters and so it is true to say that Prophet Mohammed is the 'Father of no man'.

The problem comes with the next line 'the Seal of the Prophets'. The word 'seal' in Arabic refers to a ring that is used for sealing documents and it is on this basis that certain Muslims have concluded that there can be no prophet after Prophet Mohammed. This is, of course, a possible interpretation of what was intended by the use of the word 'Seal' and perhaps even a logical one too. However, to come to this conclusion on the strength of this one word alone and to be sufficiently convinced of its meaning as to justify putting twenty thousand people to death is another matter entirely.

But there is another problem with this interpretation and this lies with the word that is used for 'prophet'. In Arabic there are two words that are commonly used, 'Nabi' and 'Rasul', and both have the meaning of prophet. There is, however, an important difference between the two. The word 'Nabi' relates to the 'Naba' or 'Judgement Day'. 'Nabi' is the word used in this context and it is appropriate because it refers to the fact that Prophet Mohammed is the last prophet of the Adamic cycle which ends with the Day of Judgement. It is perfectly correct to say, therefore, that Prophet Mohammed is the last 'Nabi' and that there can be no other 'Nabi' after him. The other word for prophet, 'Rasul', is the more general term and has no connotations of Judgement Day. What the Baha'is are saying is that Baha'u'llah has ushered in an entirely new cycle, the cycle of fulfilment and the arrival of the Kingdom of God on earth, and so the term that properly applies to Baha'u'llah is 'Rasul' and not 'Nabi'. At no time did Prophet Mohammed say that he was the last 'Rasul'.

Hardly a day goes by that I do not thank my lucky stars for having been born into a culture of reason and moderation that does not think it legitimate to kill another human being simply because he happens to think differently from myself. Such, however, is mainstream Iranian culture. Consolation can be sought in the knowledge that the messenger of God has always appeared in the worst place on earth and the reason for this, as it has been explained in the Baha'i Writings, is that even the most fanatical and savage of human beings is of great concern to the One who created us. Hard to believe, I know, but then, He has always specialised in turning around drunks, liars, adulterers and murderers and using them for His purposes. Just check out the Old Testament if you do not believe me. The Great Being is no respecter of persons, no-one is too wretched, nor too noble either for that matter, to be used to good effect. And added to this is His wish for people to know that the power of love is all-conquering, even of barbarians, and that this should be our modus operandi from now on.

Despite every conceivable effort on the part of the Iranian authorities to wipe out the 'Baha'i sect', as they call it, the Baha'i Faith which is a peaceful, tolerant, non-violent, independent religion is now firmly established in every part of the world and is growing rapidly. The fanaticism of the Iranian clergy merely serves to fan its flame. The more they seek to extinguish it, the brighter it burns.

Chapter Seventeen

A RELIGION FOR TODAY

The Baha'i Faith is all about unity, unity in diversity. It teaches that there is only one God, one religion and one race of people. It sees the earth as one country and mankind as its citizens. It confidently asserts that the unity of the world is not only desirable but inevitable.

The difference between the Baha'i Faith and political and philosophical movements that aspire to the same goal is that the founder of the Baha'i Faith is a messenger of God, or what Baha'is prefer to call a 'Manifestation' of God, and that through his words the spiritual power that is needed to bring this unity about has been made available. Baha'is believe that all the earth-shaping developments that have taken place in our world since the middle of the nineteenth century, and they are truly staggering in their range and their profusion, can be traced back to 22nd May 1844. The revelation of Baha'u'llah is seen as the epicentre of every good thing that has happened since that time and these are just the very first days of mankind's newly acquired maturity in an era that is destined to last for five hundred thousand years. If we reflect upon what has been achieved so far over the past one hundred and seventy years and then project this trend forward for the duration of the Baha'i era then we might gain just a glimpse of the marvels that lie in store for us.

I have explained that certain conditions – economic decline and environmental degradation being the main ones - are forcing us into a corner where we have to think and act collectively to find a way out. No one can go it alone because we are all dependent upon each other for our survival. This is the nature of the Day of Judgement. The days of our custodianship of Planet Earth during which we did with it as we pleased are drawing to a close and the law of God is about to take over. This is the 'Kingdom come on Earth as it is in Heaven' that Christians have been praying for. We have been given just enough rope to hang ourselves and we have made a pretty good job of it. In brief we have 'blown it' and now it is time to hand over to a higher authority.

The only way forward now is for the entire human race to come together as one and to work as a team. There can be no individual solutions to a collective problem; there can only be collective solutions to collective problems. But it has to be a genuinely collective effort and one that derives from the grassroots. What we are talking about is the rebuilding of the world from the bottom up and we have been given the necessary tools to do the job. We can forget about political leaders. They have nothing to offer the world at this stage; they are impotent to bring about the kind of change that is needed. They may fret and strut their stuff on stage a while longer but soon they will be gone and no-one will be any the worse for their going. The formidable force that derives from a critical mass of right-thinking, right-believing and right-acting citizens of the world guided by prayer and working together in unison is all that is needed.

None of this would be possible without access to the secret ingredient of the divine spirit. Without this these words would be no more than platitudes that everyone has heard a million times before and came to nothing. The secret ingredient that I am talking about is none other than the same divine spirit that reached out to me that night in my room in Liverpool in 1975 which transformed my life in a second and turned the world into a paradise. From the moment this happens, and it can and will happen for each and every one of us, we will never be the same again. Of course no-one ever becomes perfect overnight, nor is this to be expected because perfection is endless but at least we will know what perfection is and we will aspire towards it. We will strive to become better people and we will have the power to achieve it so that when some kind soul says to us 'Man, your life is a total mess!', we can reply in all honesty, 'My friend, if you think my life is a total mess now you should have seen me a year ago!'

Each day will be filled with joy and happiness, our hearts will be singing from early morning to late at night. We will sleep well and our health will improve. Whatever reason we may have had for drinking to excess or taking drugs will leave us. Each one of us will be free to become the person that he is capable of being without hindrance. This is the nature of the Baha'i experience and it is there for everyone to enjoy. There is no one who can prevent you from becoming the person you are meant to be. It is yours for the taking.

Such is the nature of the transformation that can take place in our personal lives. Now let us look at what the Baha'i teachings have to say about how we should organise ourselves as a society. But before we do let us just remind ourselves of the *Golden Rule* and acknowledge that it is a universal ethic that underpins the values of all people everywhere. It is good to remember that there is much common ground between us and that we are not and never have been very far apart.

- What is hateful to you, do not to your fellow man. That is the entire Law; all the rest is commentary. *Judaism*

- Hurt not others in ways that you yourself would find hurtful. *Buddhism*

- Do unto others as you would have them do unto you. *Christianity*

- Regard your neighbour's gain as your own gain; regard your neighbour's loss as your own loss. *Taoism*

- If one strives to treat others as he would be treated by them he will come near the perfect life. *Confucianism*

- No one of you is a believer until he desires for his brother that which he desires for himself. *Islam*

- As thou deemest thyself, so deem others. *Sikhism*

- Blessed is he who preferreth his brother before himself. *Baha'i Faith*

Although they are not carved in stone Baha'is like to make mention of these twelve basic principles:

1.   The Oneness of the world of humanity.

2.   The independent investigation of truth.

3.   The foundation of all religions is one.

4.   Religion must be the source of unity.

5.   Religion and science must be in harmony.

6.   Equality of the sexes.

7.   Religious and racial prejudice must be overcome.

8.   Universal Peace.

9.   Universal education.

10. A spiritual solution to economic problems.

11. A universal auxiliary language.

12. An international parliament of men.

Let us review these twelve principles and comment on them briefly as appropriate.

The cornerstone of Baha'i belief is unity. There is only one God and it is the same God of all the religions. There can only ever be one because as the Islamic saying goes, 'if there are two gods neither is God'. Divisions are man-made. No messenger of God has ever refuted what another religion had to say; on the contrary each has confirmed the message of his predecessors. The human race is also one. This is now accepted as a scientific fact; there do not exist two human races. The revealed word of Baha'u'llah has brought revolutionary changes to our ability to communicate and this, for the first time in our history, has made the functional unity of the whole human race a possibility. Before this our unity was not possible even when nations were living at peace.

There is no clergy in the Baha'i Faith. In former times when illiteracy was common people were in need of someone who could read and explain the holy texts to them. This is no longer the case. Each person today has a responsibility to investigate the truth for himself and no one has a right to tell another what to believe. Baha'i society is run by councils or assemblies of nine members which are elected annually by secret ballot in an atmosphere of prayer. No electioneering or canvassing is permitted. Any Baha'i over the age of twenty one years of age is eligible for election to an assembly. The Baha'i administration has three tiers, the local, the national, and the international. The latter, the Universal House of Justice which is situated on Mount Carmel in Haifa, Israel is elected for a five-year term. Baha'is believe that their administrative order is the fulfilment of Isaiah's prediction that *the government shall be upon his shoulders*.

The purpose of religion is to unite. The Baha'i writings express the concept in these words:

'Ye are the leaves of one tree and the fruits of one branch. Deal ye with one another with the utmost love and harmony, with friendliness and fellowship....So powerful is the light of unity that it can envelop the whole earth.'

'The wellbeing of mankind, its peace and security, are unattainable unless and until its unity is firmly established.'

If religion does not unite but causes schism instead, then mankind is better off without it.

Religion and science must be in harmony. If science proves something to be true then religion must accept it. To do otherwise would be superstition. The two are not contradictory. That they may have appeared so in the past has been the result of ignorance and prejudice. The principle of the independent investigation of truth will ensure that the mistakes of the past are not repeated.

Men and women are seen to be equal in the Baha'i Faith. The Persian woman named Tahirih mentioned in Chapter Thirteen who proclaimed that the emancipation of women was an unstoppable force and was executed as a consequence was one of the early followers of the Bab. Women must be given the same opportunities to develop their potential as men. It is recommended that if a family only has enough money to educate one child, then priority should be given to a girl over a boy because the mother is the first educator of the children and to educate a girl is to ensure the future education of both boys and girls. Such a recommendation contradicts the practice in most developing countries today where priority is given to a boy.

Baha'is often use the image of the 'bird of humanity' to convey the concept of gender equality. The bird of humanity has two wings, the one is male and the other is female. A bird that only has one wing or has one wing that is bigger than the other cannot fly. Given that the bird of humanity is one, then it follows that for the man to achieve his full potential the woman must achieve hers also. The one cannot progress without the other. I have found this image to be extremely effective when working in African villages and addressing the twin issues of gender based violence and women's equality. I am sure that it would work equally well in any pre-literate society anywhere in the world. Instead of entering into long and laborious discussions about human rights and the history of the Suffragette movement you simply provide this image.

Thereafter a wife only has to say to her husband, '...and don't forget, the bird of humanity has two wings.' And so it does, and it is difficult to argue with a fact like that!

Prejudice of all kinds has been progressively eroded over the past hundred years. The barriers of class, race and religion are increasingly coming under attack as people become more enlightened and understand that society's needs must be met by people with relevant skills regardless of who they are. Those who adhere to entrenched views that deny the capability of a particular group to perform as well as another are finding themselves increasingly isolated and their position increasingly untenable. Racial harmony in particular has seen enormous progress in the past fifty years in many parts of the world. The beauty of a garden comes more from the variety of its flowers than the perfection of a single species.

'God maketh no distinction between the white and the black. If the hearts are pure both are acceptable unto Him. God is no respecter of persons on account of either colour or race. All colours are acceptable to Him, be they white, black or yellow'. Abdul Baha, son of Baha'u'llah.

Baha'is believe that Baha'u'llah is the Mighty Counsellor, the Prince of Peace that the Prophet Isaiah spoke of, and Baha'is themselves are pacifists. At the same time it is recognised that in the past it has often been necessary for people to take up arms to protect themselves. Prophet Mohammed and his followers were compelled to do so and had they not done so would have been completely destroyed. However we are now entering a new era in which universal peace is attainable and violence and contention no longer have a place. People will have learned to subdue their baser instincts and the provocations and injustices that so bedevilled and destabilised our lives in the past will be eliminated. This is the day in which 'swords shall be beaten into ploughshares'.

Each person is seen as a mine rich in priceless gems that is in need of education to bring them to the surface and cause them to shine. Each and every one of us has gifts and talents and it is the role of education to identify what these gifts and talents are and to help us develop them. Education must be made available to every single person without exception. The individual is in need of education for his or her own development just as society is in need of the skills that he or she has to offer.

We have already considered at some length the relationship between spirituality and economics and there is no need to revisit the subject now. Suffice it to say that there are no political or economic solutions to our present economic crisis and that the situation will only improve when we choose as a race to conduct ourselves with commensurate integrity.

It has been obvious for some good while now that the world is in need of a common language so that we may travel to any part of it and feel at home without the encumbrance of having to make use of a dictionary or a translator. The presence of a common language will also lead to greater understanding between peoples. The Baha'i writings contain no suggestion as to what this universal language might be, except to say that it could be an existing language or it could be a new one devised for the purpose. The point is made, however, that a single person is not capable of creating this new language given the many complexities and subtleties involved and that any manufactured language would necessarily call for a large number of inputs from different sources.

Concerning the International Parliament of Man, Baha'u'llah says the following:

'The Great Being, wishing to reveal the prerequisites of the peace and tranquillity of the world and the advancement of its peoples, hath written: the Time must come when the *imperative necessity for the holding of a vast, an all-embracing assemblage of men will be universally realised. The rulers and kings of the earth must needs attend it, and, participating in its deliberations, must consider such ways and means as will lay the foundations of the world's Great Peace amongst men. Such a peace demandeth that the Great Powers should resolve, for the sake of the tranquillity of the peoples of the earth, to be fully reconciled among themselves. Should any king take up arms against another, all should unitedly arise and prevent him. If this is done, the nations of the world will no longer require any armaments, except for the purpose of preserving the security of their realms and of maintaining internal order within their territories. This will ensure the peace and composure of every people, government and nation.'*

I will leave the final word with Shoghi Effendi, the great grandson of Baha'u'llah:

'A world community in which all the economic barriers will have been permanently demolished and the interdependence of Capital and Labour recognised; in which the clamour of religious fanaticism and strife will have been forever stilled; in which the flame of racial animosity will have been finally extinguished; in which a single code of international law – the product of the considered judgement of the world's federated representatives – shall have at its sanction the instant and coercive intervention of the combined forces of the federated units; and finally a world community in which the fury of a capricious and militant nationalism will have been transmuted into an abiding consciousness of world citizenship – such indeed, appears, in its broadest outline, the Order anticipated by Baha'u'llah, an Order that shall come to be regarded as the fairest fruit of a slowly maturing age'.

And with these few words, my dear fellow citizens of the world, I rest my case!

The Citadel of Akka where Baha'u'llah and His family and a small group of followers were imprisoned from 1868 to 1870

The Universal House of Justice, Mount Carmel, Haifa

Shrine of the Bab, Mount Carmel, Haifa

A Baha'i gathering Haifa, Israel

The author, left, and Hooman re-unite in June 2011

POST SCRIPT

While I was writing this book it seemed that every time I switched on the radio to listen to the BBC World Service, which is my favourite media source by far, I would hear a piece of information that was relevant to what I was thinking about at the time, whether it was the size of the United States' 17 trillion dollar debt or the latest discovery in archaeology that has pushed our origins back to ten million years ago. This synchronicity encouraged me to keep going during moments when the cause seemed lost.

I thought long and hard about whether I should approach the delicate subject of the need to bring religion back into our lives obliquely so as not to offend anyone, or head-on at the risk of offending everyone. As you can see I have opted for the latter. Now that the book is completed I am not sorry that I did. I have said repeatedly that time is too short to do anything other than get straight to the point.

To those who may be angered by what I have to say I make no apologies. If our world continues to disintegrate, as I expect it to, then I would ask you to kindly re-read the book and reflect again on its content. And if the world does not continue to disintegrate, then by all means come back to me and tell me to keep my thoughts to myself. And of course there is always a possibility that it might not. Indeed, I sincerely hope that it does not and that I am wrong.

BIBLIOGRAPHY

The Secret of Divine Civilisation	Abdul Baha
The Reality of Man	Abdul Baha
Thief in the Night	William Sears
Buddhism and the Baha'i Faith	Moojan Momen
Hinduism and the Baha'i Faith	Moojan Momen
Baha'u'llah: A Short Biography	Moojan Momen
The Golden Rule	H.T.D. Rost
God Passes By	Shoghi Effendi
Muhammed and the Course of Islam	Hasan Balyuzi
Without Syllable or Sound	Michael Sours
Baha'u'llah and the New Era	John Esslemont

ABOUT THE AUTHOR

Richard Poole grew up in Bristol where he attended Begbrook Primary School and Fairfield Grammar School before moving to Southampton to study modern languages. He later completed a Master's degree in the political and economic history of Peru at Liverpool University. After serving as a volunteer in Ecuador he decided to make humanitarian assistance his career and subsequently worked with a number of different non-governmental organisations including Voluntary Service Overseas of the UK, International Voluntary Services Inc. and the American Refugee Committee of the USA, and Trocaire of Ireland. Altogether he has spent over thirty years working in emergency, reconstruction and development in Africa, Latin America and the Caribbean. The projects have included agricultural development, reforestation, primary health care, water and sanitation, and micro-credit in settled communities, as well as life support for IDPs and refugees.

He is especially proud of the year that he spent playing professional football in Ecuador as a member of the Liga Deportiva Universitaria squad that won the national championship in 1969.

Richard is the author of four books which seek to share with others the immense passion, joy and satisfaction of his experiences as a humanitarian worker.

Today he is based in Colchester UK and works as an international consultant in relief and development. He has recently returned from Rwanda where he managed a camp of 19,000 Congolese Tutsi refugees.

BOOKS

O is a symbol of the world, of oneness and unity. In different cultures it also means the "eye," symbolizing knowledge and insight. We aim to publish books that are accessible, constructive and that challenge accepted opinion, both that of academia and the "moral majority."

Our books are available in all good English language bookstores worldwide. If you don't see the book on the shelves ask the bookstore to order it for you, quoting the ISBN number and title. Alternatively you can order online (all major online retail sites carry our titles) or contact the distributor in the relevant country, listed on the copyright page.

See our website **www.o-books.net** for a full list of over 500 titles, growing by 100 a year.

And tune in to myspiritradio.com for our book review radio show, hosted by June-Elleni Laine, where you can listen to the authors discussing their books.